Religion in focus

Islam

in today's world

Claire Clinton

Sally Lynch

Janet Orchard

Deborah Weston

Angela Wright

John Murray

Other titles in this series:
Christianity in today's world ISBN 0 7195 7193 6
Judaism in today's world ISBN 0 7195 7197 9

The Qur'an and the Hadith

In this book you will find many quotations from the Qur'an and the Hadith. You can find explanations of the importance for Muslims of these on pages 8 and 9 and in the Glossary. The Qur'an followed by the Hadith are the highest sources of authority for Muslims. We have used a simplified form of Abdullah Yusuf Ali's translation of the Qur'an.

We have used a variety of translations of the Hadith. You will notice that we have quoted from one collection of Hadith more frequently than any other. This is the collection of Muhammad al-Bukhari (died 870CE), captioned 'Bukhari Hadith', one of those most widely accepted by the Muslim communities in Britain. The references we give are in the form 'Book. Individual hadith'. Three-part references (not used here) refer to 'Volume: Book. Individual hadith'. You will see that we have not been able to complete all of the references for the Hadith quotations. If you can provide any of these, please write to the Publisher, who will be very grateful to hear from you.

Other sources

In this book you will also find many contemporary statements about Muslim beliefs.

> Statements presented like this, in this typeface, in a word bubble, are the views of ordinary Muslims, mostly British Muslims. They would not necessarily be seen as authoritative by Muslims.

※ This Arabic 'logo-type' is composed of the words 'Sallallahu alaihi wa-sallam', sometimes written as (SAW), which means 'The blessing of Allah be upon him and peace.' These words are used by Muslims every time the Prophet Muhammad ※ is mentioned. When other prophets are named Muslims say 'Alaihi as sallam' – 'Peace be upon him'.

Note: Words printed in SMALL CAPITALS (first mention only) are defined in the Glossary on pages 120–21.

With thanks to

Many members of the Muslim faith community in Britain and representatives of many different Muslim organisations have been consulted in the preparation of this book. However, the authors take full responsibility for the views expressed herein. The authors would particularly like to acknowledge the helpful advice of the following:

Maqsood Ahmad Director, Kirklees Racial Equality Council; **Akbarali Amaneer** teacher; **Dr Zaki Badawi** Principal of The Muslim College, London; **Lat Blaylock** Executive Officer of the Professional Council for Religious Education; **Sophie Chisty** student; **Surayah Gramy** RE Teacher; **Janet Dyson** Education Inspector, Essex; **Dr Suhaib Hasan** and **Khola Husan** of The Islamic Shari'a Council, London E10; **Fazlun Khalid** Founder and Director of the Islamic Foundation for Ecology and Environmental Sciences; **Akram Khan-Cheema** Educational Consultant; **Mrs Morali** The World Federation of Shia Ithna-Asheri Muslim Communities; **Hassan Morrison** The Islamic Awareness and Education Project; **Roger Owen** GCSE Chief Examiner; **Abdul Qayum** Imam, East London Mosque; **Mr Roganiha** The Iranian News Agency; **Moona Taslim-Saif** Taslim Funerals; **Sarah Sheriff** and **Zarina** Muslim Women's Helpline; **Abu Syed** teacher; **Ahmed Versi** Editor, Muslim News; as well as other unnamed individuals whose constructive criticism throughout the development of this book has helped to shape our approach. Finally, we thank our teaching colleagues and families who have helped and supported us through the writing of this material.

© Claire Clinton, Sally Lynch, Janet Orchard, Deborah Weston, Angela Wright 1999

First published in 1999
by John Murray (Publishers) Ltd
50 Albemarle Street
London W1S 4BD

Reprinted 1999, 2001

Artwork by Oxford Illustrators Ltd
Layouts by Fiona Webb
Typeset in Rockwell Light by Wearset, Boldon, Tyne and Wear
Printed and bound in Italy by G Canale, Torino

A CIP record for this book is available from the British Library.

ISBN 0 7195 7194 4

Teacher's Book ISBN 0 7195 7432 3

Contents

Acknowledgements

The authors and publishers are grateful to the following for permission to include material in the text:

pp.6–7 *Trends*; **p.13** from *What Muslims believe*, Ed. John Bowker, published by Oneworld Publications; **pp.18–19** *1994 Annual Report of the Helpline* and *A Small Kindness* published by the Muslim Women's Helpline; **p.32** *Trends*; **p.45** *Trends*; **p.58** the *Independent on Sunday*; **p.70** *Women in Islam* by Aisha Lemu and Fatima Heeren; **pp.84–5** *A Small Kindness* published by the Muslim Women's Helpline; **p.86** Ahmed Versi © The *Guardian*; **p.87** *Women in Islam* by Aisha Lemu and Fatima Heeren; **p.88** *Trends*; **pp.94–5** from *The Autobiography of Malcolm X*, with assistance from Alex Haley, published by Penguin Books; **pp.102–3** *Trends*.

Photo acknowledgements

Cover A. Abbas/Magnum; **p.1** The British Library (Ms. Add. 4810); **p.2** courtesy Hassan Morrison; **p.3** *t* Peter Sanders, *b* Muhsin Kilby; **p.4** Brian Bahr/Allsport; **p.5** courtesy The Dream Foundation, Houston, Texas; **p.6** Ahmed Versi/Muslim News; **p.7** courtesy *Trends* magazine; **p.9** *t* courtesy Islamic Computing, *b* Peter Sanders; **p.16** *tl & tr* Peter Sanders, *b* Muhsin Kilby; **p.17** *t* Muhsin Kilby, *b* Peter Sanders; **p.20** Ahmed Versi/Muslim News; **p.23** Peter Sanders; **p.25** Muhsin Kilby; **p.26** courtesy Ahmed Moustafa; **p.28** *t* Royal Society of Fine Arts, Amman, *b* Peter Sanders; **p.31** Powerstock/Zefa; **p.32** courtesy Muslim Educational Trust; **p.34** Rex Features; **p.35** Peter Sanders; **p.36** Peter Sanders; **p.38** courtesy Lord Nazir Ahmed of Rotherham; **p.39** courtesy Net Turistik Yayinlar; **p.42** courtesy Net Turistik Yayinlar; **p.44** *l* Phil Jude/Science Photo Library, *r* CNRI/Science Photo Library; **p.46** *t* © Richard Greenhill/Sally & Richard Greenhill Photo Library, *b* A. Abbas/Magnum; **p.47** courtesy Al-Hidaayah Publishing & Distribution Ltd.; **p.50** *t & b* Moona Taslim-Saif; **p.53** Peter Sanders; **p.54** Muhsin Kilby; **p.56** Network Photographers; **p.57** John Townson/Creation; **p.58** Tom Pilston/The Independent; **p.63** © *Evening Standard Magazine*; **p.64** *tl* Petit Format/Nestlé/Science Photo Library, *tr* Peter Sanders, *b* Dag Ohrlund/Rex Features; **p.65** courtesy Islamic Foundation; **p.66** *tl, bl, bc & br* Peter Sanders, *tr* Muhsin Kilby; **p.67** Peter Sanders; **p.70** *t & b* Muhsin Kilby, *c* Peter Sanders; **p.71** *tl, tr & br* Muhsin Kilby, *bl* Peter Sanders; **p.75** courtesy Dateline; **p.76** *all* Peter Sanders; **p.77** *t & b* Peter Sanders; **p.79** Newsteam International; **p.81** *logo* courtesy The Islamic Shari'a Council; **p.87** *t & b* Muhsin Kilby, *c* Peter Sanders; **p.88** Muhsin Kilby; **p.89** courtesy Maqsood Ahmad; **p.90** courtesy Maqsood Ahmad; **p.92** courtesy Maqsood Ahmad; **p.94** PA News Photo Library; **p.96** Deborah Weston; **p.97** courtesy Islamic Foundation for Ecology and Environmental Sciences (IFEES); **p.99** *tl, tr & bl* courtesy Muslim Aid, *br* Muhsin Kilby; **p.100** *t* J. Sutton Hibbert/Rex Features, *logo, bl & br* courtesy Muslim Aid; **p.101** *l & r* courtesy Muslim Aid; **p.102** *t* John Townson/Creation, *b* Jim Belben; **p.104** *tl* Ian West/Oxford Scientific Films, *tr* Ronald Toms/Oxford Scientific Films, *b* Richard Packwood/Oxford Scientific Films; **p.107** © Clive Shirley/Panos Pictures; **p.108** Mike Brown/Oxford Scientific Films; **p.109** WWF/Hans J. Burkard/Bilderberg; **p.110** Peter Sanders; **p. 116** *logo & photo* © Open House/Amos Trust; **p.117** courtesy Muslim Aid.

t = top, *l* = left, *r* = right, *b* = bottom, *c* = centre.

While every effort has been made to contact copyright holders, the publishers apologise for any omissions, which they will be pleased to rectify at the earliest opportunity.

UNIT 1

An Islamic world view

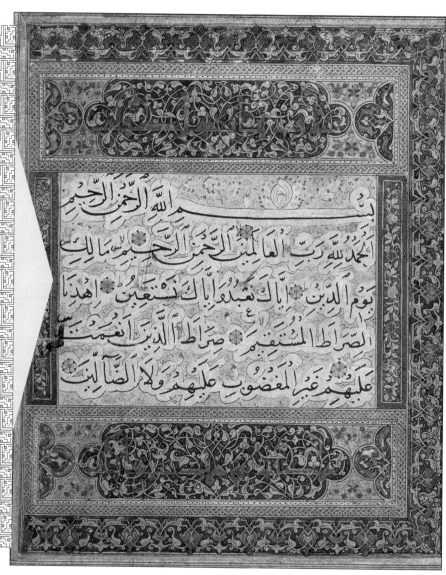

In the name of Allah,
Most Gracious,
Most Merciful.

Praise be to Allah,
The Cherisher and Sustainer
 of the Worlds;

Most Gracious,
Most Merciful;
Master of the Day
 of Judgement.

It is You that we worship
And to You alone do we
 turn for help.

Show us the straight way,
The way of those people
To whom You have shown
 Your Grace,
Those who have not made
 You Angry
And do not go astray.

SURAH 1 (based on the translation of the Qur'an by Abdullah Yusuf Ali)

This is the first SURAH (division) of the QUR'AN. It is called AL-FATIHAH, which means
'The Opening'. All Muslims learn these words by heart in the Arabic language
and recite them every time they pray.

For Muslims, Al-Fatihah expresses some of the most important ideas about
ALLAH, and about each Muslim's relationship to Allah.

In this introductory unit you will get an overview of these big ideas of Islam.

1.1 What does Al-Fatihah mean to Muslims?

Al-Fatihah sums up the core beliefs of Islam.

- Muslims believe Allah is the **one God**, who gave them life. (Allah is the word for God in Arabic.) Only Allah should be worshipped.
- They see the wonders of the natural world as the work of Allah **the Creator**.
- They believe that Allah will **judge** all people after they die. Every deed is recorded. If people do more good than bad in their life they will be rewarded with **paradise**. If they do more bad than good, then **hell** will be their punishment.
- They believe Allah is merciful and compassionate.
- They believe Allah has provided guidance for humankind.

In Sources A and B two British Muslims comment on Al-Fatihah.

A

I think that it is a brilliant idea to start your book with Al-Fatihah. It is the most basic, most important statement in Islam. Get all your readers to learn it! . . .

It is very important to me as a human being that I turn only to Allah for help, that I don't go for help to anything Allah has made. I worship Him alone; I don't worship any part of His Creation, such as a tree or a stone.

From an interview with Hassan Morrison, who worked for the Post Office for fourteen years before he was a Muslim. Now he works for The Islamic Awareness and Education Project, which aims to help teachers present Islam in schools by arranging for visits by Muslim speakers and providing background information.

B

We thought, what better than to call our company Al-Fatihah, after this opening chapter of the Qur'an? Our work is about the beginning, opening up children's lives, opening up their understanding of religion, Islam and education . . .

Al-Fatihah makes everybody aware that Allah is the Creator and everything stems from that. When we understand this completely we are more able to implement the rest of Islam in our lives; we know about our Creator, and that He has made us, our nature and our environment.

From an interview with Nilufa who runs a company called Al-Fatihah Educational Aids, which organises Islamic parenting seminars and also supplies written materials. She explains why she named her company after this surah.

SAVE AS . . .

1 Hassan Morrison suggests everyone learns Al-Fatihah. It may help you in your exam if you can quote it from memory. It will take you only a few minutes to learn. Your teacher can give you advice on how to do it.

C

*It is right and wise—
To believe in Allah
And the Last Day,
And the Angels,
And the Book
And the Prophets;*

*To spend part of your
    savings
Because you love Him
For your relations,
For orphans,
For the needy,
For the traveller,
For those who ask,
And for buying the
    freedom of slaves;*

*To be steadfast in prayer,
And to practise charity
    regularly,
To fulfil the contracts
    which you have made;
And to be firm and
    patient,
In pain or suffering
And in times of worry,
And throughout all
    periods of panic.*

*Such are the people of
    truth, those who fear
    Allah.*

Surah 2.177

The straight way

When Muslims say Al-Fatihah they call on Allah to show them 'the straight way'. This is the way Allah wants all people to live.

So what is 'the straight way'? That is what this book is all about, and it cannot be summed up in a few words. All through their lives, Muslims are learning about which way is the straight way. However, Source C is one of the most important pointers. It comes from the Qur'an.

D

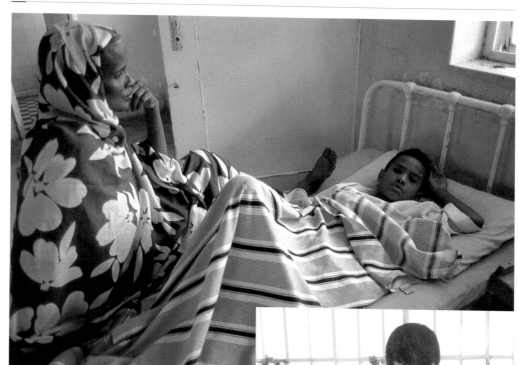

A mother by her sick child's bedside in Sudan

E

An orphanage set up by Muslims in Hebron

FOCUS TASK

1   Copy this table. Use Al-Fatihah and Sources A–C to complete it.

Beliefs of a good Muslim	Actions of a good Muslim

2   Write longer captions for Sources D and E explaining how you think these Muslims are following the guidance in Source C.

Not just a religion, but a whole way of life

Abdul Hakeem Olajuwon is one of the world's greatest basketball players. He was born in Lagos, Nigeria, then moved to the USA as a teenager. He now plays for the Rockets in Houston, Texas. In 1998 his earnings were estimated to be £12 million.

Abdul Hakeem is a Muslim. You will see from this interview that Islam runs through every aspect of his life. Islam is not only what he does in a mosque or at prayer, but it is also how he behaves on the basketball field or at home with his wife and family. Islam affects everything Abdul Hakeem does, thinks and feels.

WORK

Basketball is secondary; everything is secondary when it comes to Islam. There is no separation between my religion and my work. A Muslim looks at his work, not as a job, but as part of his religious duty. This for me means being responsible in working out and training. It is part of worship. So you get the reward just as you do if you went to pray. It is the same because the intention is the same.

Work is part of your religious duty that you must do to support your family. There is no separation – everything goes back to please God.

> You will learn about the Qur'an on pages 8 and 32.

> This belief is called IBADAH. You will learn about this on pages 12–13.

RESPONSIBILITY

Islam is a religion of peace. It is the responsibility of every Muslim to reflect Islam in their life. You don't have to talk about it; if people see Islam they admire it because there is so much beauty and love and passion. In Islam you see it – you see equality, you see justice.

The Qur'an has four 'rights' on every Muslim: first of all we must learn to recite the Qur'an. We must understand it correctly, that is the second 'right'. The third one is that we must apply its laws in our life. Then the fourth is that we must teach it to others.

PRAYER

Sometimes the sunset prayer is at eight, so I look for an opportunity to pray during the game. Say there's a time out, I just run to join some of my friends who are watching the game when they go for prayer. Then I run back out. People don't even know – they see me go to the locker room without realising what I am doing.

> This duty is called SALAH. You will learn about this on pages 13 and 36.

TESTING

In the NBA championship against the New York Knicks in 1994, it was game seven in a seven-game series and it was tied, 3–3. I went to prayer before the game as usual, but I look at the whole situation as a test for me. I love to win the championships, but only if it is meant to be; if it is God's will and if it is best for me to win – God knows best. So I was willing to win or lose as long as I did my best out there. That was my attitude going to the game. After the game, which we won, the team realised that I was ready to submit either way and to see that as the victory. Afterwards you just take time out to glorify and to thank Allah for His decision and for giving me this opportunity, to accomplish this or receive this reward.

> You will learn about life being a test on page 44.

ISLAM NEWSFILE

Islam and Muslims are constantly in the news. Later in this course you will do an analysis of how the newspapers cover Muslim stories compared to how they portray other religions. As you work through the course, collect as a class any newspaper coverage of Muslims and other religions you can find.

You will learn about women in Islam on pages 84-8.

You will learn about Muslim attitudes to abortion on pages 53-5.

You will learn about Allah on pages 24-39.

FAMILIES

Living in the West, I see women fighting for equality, fighting for respect. They cannot get it because they are not going about it the right way. Muslim women don't have to fight for it because Allah has given it to them in law. It is the duty of every Muslim man to respect the law of Allah.

In Islam, women are regarded as our mothers, our wives and our daughters, our sisters: family.

The man is the head of the family and the woman is its heart. These two, head and heart, are not in competition. They are not equal because they have different functions. When women in the West talk about equality they mean the same function; they have misunderstood equality. That is why there are so many problems.

I have a wife called Dalia and two children. Both of us love children, we would love to have more, we do not budget kids as they do over here. Allah

says in the Qur'an, 'Do not kill your children or abort them because He (Allah) will take care of you and them.' So it is not you that is taking care of them, you just have to trust God and let things go naturally, without trying to control. We take children as a blessing.

RACE

The example of the Prophet (Peace be Upon Him), which we try to follow, means no black superiority or white superiority. According to him, you enter into any relationship as an equal. I don't look at myself as a Nigerian or an American. I look at myself as a Muslim.

DOUBT AND BELIEF

My full first name is Abdul Hakeem, which means 'the servant of the Most Wise'. Allah is the Most Wise. I have never doubted my religion because it is natural. Islam is a natural way. It applies to your nature.

It points you to look at the universe and look at creation. Behind all this creation there is a Creator, and this is the Creator that you serve. Any other that you put beside this Creator is false. All the power is with the Creator, so Islam encourages us to submit to the Creator, not the creation. Everything in the universe submits and surrenders to this One. That is why there is no doubt in the religion, because you know there is only One.

You will learn about Muslim attitudes to global issues on pages 97-117.

You will learn about Muslim attitudes to marriage and the family on pages 72-83.

You will learn about Muslim attitudes to race on pages 89-95.

ACTIVITY

Work in groups.
1 **Brainstorm all the questions you have about Islam. Abdul Hakeem's comments may raise some questions for you. What other questions about Islam would you like this course to answer?**
2 **Write each question on a separate slip of paper.**
3 **Sort these questions into categories. You could use general categories such as Muslim beliefs and Muslim actions. Or you could sort your questions by subject, such as prayer, worship, relationships, attitudes, etc. As you work through this course, refer back to these questions every now and then to see how far you have answered them.**

SAVE AS ...

4 **Do you expect your study of Islam in today's world to be relevant to your own life?**
a) On a scale of 1 to 5, say how relevant you expect it to be.

Not relevant | 1 2 3 4 5 | Very relevant

b) Write a paragraph to explain your answer.

Later in this course you will see if your views have changed at all.

1.2 How do Muslims find out how Allah wants them to live?

Islam makes no distinction between the sacred and the secular. It is a complete way of life. Newcomers to the Qur'an and HADITH are often surprised at the clear advice they contain about everyday life. So sometimes it is easy for Muslims to know what is right and good. At other times it is more difficult, particularly when the modern world throws up new opportunities or new temptations. In such situations Muslims need to go back to their sources of authority to form a judgement on what is right and good. On the next six pages we will look at how Muslims do this.

How did Dr Darsh arrive at his advice?

Until his death in 1997, Sheikh Syed Darsh was Chairman of the Islamic Shari'a Council in the UK, which was set up to solve the marriage problems of British Muslims according to Islamic family law. The Council is made up of members from all the major Muslim groups.

Dr Darsh was highly respected among British Muslims, who often asked his opinion on moral issues. Source A contains edited extracts from an advice page he wrote on marriage and relationships.

ACTIVITY

1   Read Source A carefully. Find one example of Dr Darsh using each of the following sources of authority. You could record your answers in a chart like this.

Source of Authority	Example
The Qur'an	
Hadith (stories about or sayings of Muhammad ﷺ)	
SHARI'AH (Islamic law)	
Other (e.g. customs or traditions)	

2   Which source is used most often? Try to explain why you think it is used most often. Don't worry if this is difficult. These are only your first ideas.

3   Choose one piece of Dr Darsh's advice on marriage with which you agree and one piece with which you disagree and explain your choice.

A

Can a girl/boy choose her/his own partner?

Traditionally it was left to families who knew one another to arrange a proposal. Islam has given each party the right to see the other in a family setting. If they like one another, the match may go further and marriage preparations proceed.

As far as the girl is concerned, the messenger of Allah has given her the right to express her views on the proposed person. In the hadith he said, 'The permission of the virgin is to be sought. And if she does not object, her silence is her permission.' This is the traditional old-fashioned way.

Nowadays girls go to schools and proceed to universities. They are mature, well educated, cultured and outspoken. These factors have to be taken into consideration. Parents have to realise they are not buying or selling commodities.

In the words of the hadith, 'If a person with satisfying religious attitude comes to you to seek your daughter in marriage, accept that. If you do not, there will be great mischief on earth and a great trouble.'

At the same time young people who are blessed with education have to show patience and understanding, and should argue their case in a rational and respectable manner.

What should one look for in a partner?

It is very difficult to give general guidelines, as people are individuals and as such have different priorities when selecting a lifelong partner. However, the hadith has given us some clues as to what is to be desired most in both men and women: 'A woman may be sought in marriage either for her beauty, nobility, wealth or religious inclination. Seek the last and you will be the more successful.' The same holds for the female in the choice of a partner.

Marriage is not for fun or experience. It is a lifelong relationship. For that reason, any factor detrimental to the relationship should be avoided as much as is possible. Highly educated males and females should seek partners of similar educational background. Cultural and family background is very important. Such things help

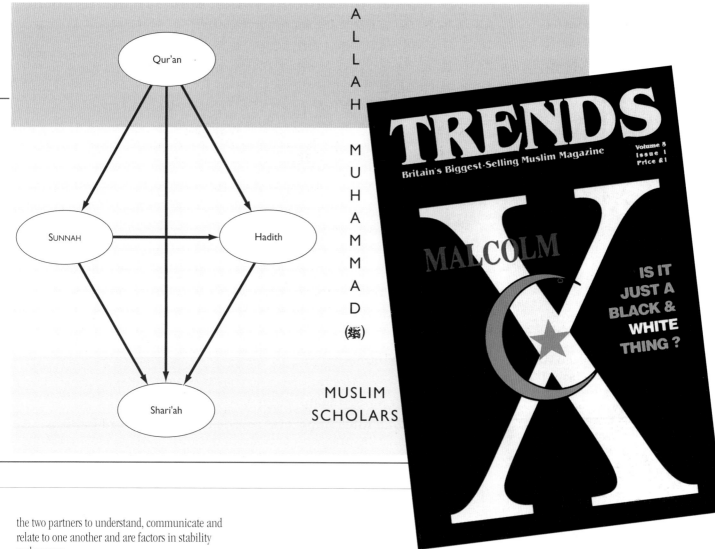

the two partners to understand, communicate and relate to one another and are factors in stability and success.

However, considering the particular position of Muslim communities living in minority situations, the most fundamental question when choosing a partner is a religious one.

Can a parent refuse a proposal from a good Muslim for his daughter on the basis that the suitor is not of the same race/caste?

There is no concept of caste in Islam. Racial background is a fact of life. The Qur'an considers the difference of race, colour or language as signs of the creative ability of Allah: 'And of His signs is the creation of the heavens and earth and the difference of your language and colours. Lo! here indeed are signs for men of knowledge.' (Qur'an 30.22)

In surah 49 verse 13 is the most universal doctrine of human equality and brotherhood: 'Oh mankind! We have created you from a male and a female, and then rendered you into nations and tribes so that you might know one another. Indeed the most honourable among you in the sight of Allah is he who is most pious.'

There is a wealth of hadith where the messenger of Allah condemned outright any racial impact on Islamic society.

But customs die hard, and this social attitude is very difficult to abolish outright. In the new environment of living in Britain the situation may ease gradually. Young people facing parental opposition in such a situation have to be patient to advance their case.

Are secret marriages allowed, e.g. where girls or boys marry without parental consent, knowledge or approval?

Muslim scholars frown upon secretive arrangements. They argue that the shari'ah has made it mandatory to publicise marriage in every available way. They quote a number of statements of the Prophet to that effect. For example the statement, 'There is no valid marriage without a guardian and two male witnesses. Any arrangement short of that is invalid, invalid, invalid.'

And Allah says the Truth and guides to the right way.

Extracts and a cover from *Trends*, the magazine most widely read by young British Muslims. Its current circulation is approximately 15,000. It has tackled issues as varied as marriage, war, education and health. You can find out about Malcolm X on pages 94–5.

How do sources of authority within Islam relate to each other?

1 Draw your own simplified copy of the diagram on page 7, like this.

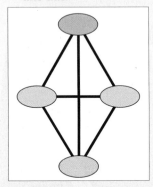

2 Add arrows, as on the page 7 diagram, then using the text on this page add labels to explain what the arrows mean. You will need to think about what the relationship is between each form of revelation. How does one lead into another?

3 Explain why there are arrows from the Qur'an to all three of the other elements.

4 Some Muslims think that they should copy literally everything that Muhammad ﷺ did. For example, Muhammad ﷺ made his welfare payments in barley – so should they.

Others believe his lifestyle gives them a model to adapt their lives to. So they pay their welfare payments in cash. How might Muslims explain their decision to:
a) copy Muhammad ﷺ literally or
b) adapt his practices to their own situation?

On pages 6 and 7 you should have found that Dr Darsh used various sources of authority to support his answers. The panels on this page describe Muslims' different sources of authority.

B

Qur'an – meaning 'recitation'

All Muslims regard the Qur'an as their most important source of authority. It was:

- revealed to MUHAMMAD ﷺ in the Arabic language over a period of 23 years
- recited by Muhammad ﷺ and memorised by him and his companions
- written down by others during Muhammad's ﷺ lifetime (570–632CE)
- collected together in Arabic and arranged in 114 surahs (divisions) after Muhammad's ﷺ death, and checked for accuracy against what many people had learned by heart.
- Some Muslims learn the entire Qur'an by heart and earn the title of HAFIZ, a very respected status.

Sunnah – meaning 'customary practices'

This is the second most important source of authority for Muslims

- Sunnah refers to the practices, customs and traditions of Muhammad ﷺ that are considered to be 'model' – a perfect example. They are found in hadith (see right) and other texts.
- Muslims try to imitate Muhammad's ﷺ life as closely as they can and regard him as a perfect human being. He is an inspiration to all Muslims.
- Muhammad ﷺ is known as the 'seal of the prophets', the last prophet, to whom Allah revealed the Qur'an.

Shari'ah – meaning 'the straight way' or 'clear straight path'

This is the Islamic law

Muslims believe that by following Shari'ah, they are living life the way that Allah wants them to. In Islam the law is based on the Qur'an and the Sunnah and is used by Muslims to make moral decisions. Some people become experts in Shari'ah. The Shari'ah explains how to put the principles of the Qur'an and Sunnah into practice. By following the Shari'ah, Muslims can live the way they believe Allah wants them to.

How do Muslims use these sources of authority?

- The first question for any Muslim on any issue is, 'What does the Qur'an say?'
- If the Qur'an does not give clear guidance, the next question is, 'What more can I find out about this from other texts?'
- The third question is, 'How have scholars interpreted all this?'

Here is an example of the way this process works in practice. How could these sources of authority help a Muslim to know how to pray?

Stage 1

What does the Qur'an say about prayer?

The Qur'an talks a lot about the importance of prayer. Again and again it instructs Muslims to pray regularly, often, and at fixed times and explains the value of prayer. But it doesn't lay down precisely how to pray or when.

Hadith – *meaning 'saying, report, account'*
This is the written record of the Sunnah

- Hadith are the sayings of Muhammad as told by his household, family and companions.
- There are different collections of hadith. Different groups of Muslims accept different collections of hadith as reliable sources of authority.

Stage 2

What more can you find out about prayer from hadith and the example of Muhammad ?

Muhammad often taught about prayer. There are clear accounts of him performing the prayers at the five set times. There are detailed descriptions of the different prayer positions he used and the words from the Qur'an he used to recite in his prayers.

Stage 3

How have scholars interpreted all this?

Different traditions have developed different ways of praying based on their interpretations of what they believe are the authoritative (genuine) accounts of Muhammad's words and deeds. Most Muslims pray five times a day, whilst others say that it is permissible to pray just three times, by joining together the midday and afternoon prayers and by joining together the evening and night prayers. Some use slightly different positions or different forms of words, but all agree that they must pray and that it is their duty to Allah to do so.

Of course, many ordinary Muslims do not go through these stages every time on every issue. They more usually learn from IMAMS (religious leaders), their parents or their teachers what to do. But the advice they receive is based on this process.

The Moral Ocean

How do *you* decide between right and wrong?

- Do you ask advice from other people?
- Do you think of what your religion or upbringing has taught you?
- Do you work out an answer for yourself?
- Do you think, 'What would happen if …?' and go for the option with the best outcome?
- Do you think, 'What would so-and-so do in this situation?' and try to follow their example?
- Do you have a different way altogether?

Your moral decisions are influenced by many different factors. These influences include other people; past experiences; significant books; friends and family. Your moral values may develop and change as you grow more knowledgeable or become wiser. And whether or not you are aware of it, your moral decisions will be influenced by the moral values of the culture around you, even if you do not accept these values.

So, making moral decisions is a little like steering a ship through dangerous or exciting unknown waters. You may have already seen an illustration of the Moral Ocean in your study of other religions. To help you reach a decision you are happy with and which you feel is right there are many islands you can visit. These islands are *your* sources of moral authority.

You have already found out about some of the main sources of authority for Muslims. You can see them and some of the many other islands which a Muslim might visit on this diagram. Do you think a Muslim's route through the ocean would be similar to or different from that of a non-Muslim?

✓ CHECKPOINT

You will need to know the meaning of these two terms:

- ABSOLUTE MORALITY – this is when a person believes that there is a right course of action in a moral dilemma that is true in all situations, regardless of culture, religious tradition, time or age. For example: 'it is always wrong to kill.'
- RELATIVE MORALITY – this is when a person has strong beliefs or principles but they believe that different courses of action might be needed in different situations. For example: 'it is usually wrong to kill, but sometimes it might be necessary for a particular reason.'

WHAT SHALL I DO?

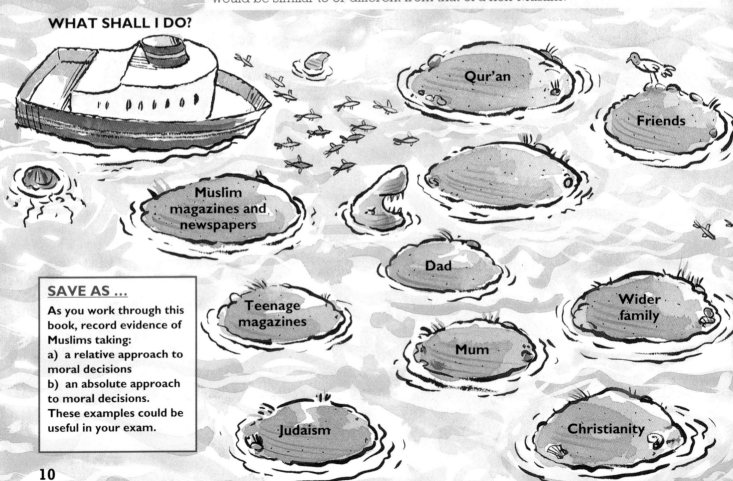

SAVE AS …

As you work through this book, record evidence of Muslims taking:
a) a relative approach to moral decisions
b) an absolute approach to moral decisions.
These examples could be useful in your exam.

Conscience

Secular wisdom

Shari'ah

Writings of Muslim scholars

Hadith

5 pillars of faith

Sunnah

DECISION I SHOULD MAKE

Muslim leaders

FOCUS TASK

1   On your own copy of this diagram, plot the route you think a Muslim would take across the Moral Ocean. They can call at five islands before making their decision. Make sure they visit their most important island first.
2   What differences, if any, are there between a Muslim's route and the route you might take? You may want to label the empty islands.

SAVE AS ...

3   What does the Muslim route say about the way Muslims make moral decisions? Use the structure below to write four paragraphs to explain the Muslim route across the Moral Ocean diagram. You will need to refer to pages 8–9.

   •   Sources of authority are ...
   •   The main sources of authority for Muslims are ...
   •   The first island a Muslim would visit ... (Explain why.)
   •   Muslims might also visit ... (Choose another two islands and explain why a Muslim would visit them.)

1.3 Islam is …

Faith and worship

IMAN means 'faith' or 'belief'. Islam has six key beliefs, which can be described as the foundation stones upon which the religion is based.

Ibadah means 'worship'. The main acts of ibadah are called 'the five pillars of Islam'. All Muslims are expected to follow Allah's instructions about them and they play an important role in a Muslim's life.

Muhammad describes the acts of ibadah and the beliefs of iman in Source A. This story is found in both of the most widely accepted collections of hadith.

A

Umar said:

'One day when we were with Allah's messenger , a man with very white clothing and very black hair came up to us. No mark of travel was visible on him, and none of us recognised him. Sitting down beside the Prophet , he said,

"Muhammad , tell me about Islam."

He replied, "Islam means that you should testify that there is no god but Allah and that Muhammad is the Messenger of Allah, that you should observe the prayer, pay the ZAKAH, fast during Ramadan, and make the pilgrimage to the KA'BAH if you have the means to go."

The man said, "You have spoken the truth."

We were surprised at his questioning Muhammad and then declaring that he spoke the truth.

The man then said, "Now tell me about iman (faith)."

Muhammad replied, "Iman means that you should believe in Allah, His angels, His books, His messengers, and the Last Day, and that you should believe in the Decree of both good and evil."

The man then said, "Now tell me about IHSAN (perfection)."

Muhammad replied, "It means that you should worship Allah as though you saw Him, for He sees you though you do not see Him." '

The stranger then left the company and Muhammad informed them it had been the angel JIBRIL, come to instruct them in matters of their religion.

Muslim Hadith 1.001. This hadith covers similar topics to the Qur'an quotation in Source C on page 3.

1 On a copy of Source A, highlight the phrases telling Muslims about worshipping Allah.
2 Compare the hadith in Source A with Source C on page 3. Would Muslims learn the same things about worship from each of these passages?
3 Is it helpful or unhelpful for Muslims to have both these sources? Discuss why.

ACTIVITY

1 Make a simple copy of this diagram.
2 Label the foundation stones on your diagram with the six key beliefs of iman mentioned by Muhammad in Source A.
3 Label the five pillars on your diagram using Source B to help you.
4 The statements in Source C show how the pillars develop the faith of a Muslim. Use them to complete the following phrase for each pillar on your diagram: 'This pillar helps Muslims to …'

B

Pillar	Description	How often (minimum)
1 SHAHADAH (declaration of faith)	The Shahadah is the statement, 'There is no god except Allah and Muhammad ﷺ is the Messenger of Allah.'	Every time a Muslim prays
2 Salah (prayer)	A way of worshipping Allah by communicating with Him. Muslims perform salah and prepare themselves for it in the particular way taught by Muhammad ﷺ (see page 36).	Five times each day
3 Zakah (welfare payment)	Giving a percentage of wealth, if you can afford it, to benefit the poor, worship Allah and purify the giver.	Annually
4 SAWM (fasting)	From just before dawn until sunset every day during the month of Ramadan, Muslims are required to go without food, drink (including water), smoking and sex.	Annually
5 HAJJ (pilgrimage to MAKKAH)	Each Muslim must complete the Hajj if he or she is healthy and can afford it.	Hajj takes place annually, but Muslims are expected to go at least once in a lifetime

C

1 When I made my Shahadah (declaration of faith) in front of a group of Muslims, I was officially a Muslim. I felt as if I immediately moved a step closer to Allah by publicly stating that obvious truth.

2 When I was a child, all I could manage was to recite the words of the Shahadah, do the prayer, give up a little food in Ramadan and put a bit of pocket money in the zakah box in the mosque. As I grow older, I can understand more of the inner meaning behind the actions. I am getting to know what Allah wants from me. I hope this means I am closer to Him now.

3 Prayer helps me to develop my consciousness of the Creator – Allah.

6 I contribute 2.5 per cent of my savings to the needy and disadvantaged in the Muslim community, and beyond. Those pillars set me on the road of sacrifice, perseverance and patience.

4 Fasting during Ramadan teaches me patience, discipline and control. Time flies by for me every day and I don't really have trouble fasting, unless I have been playing football, in which case I feel thirsty easily.

5 The Hajj is a pilgrimage, not only to Makkah but also towards my Creator, towards Allah, so that I can reflect the attributes of Allah – mercy, compassion, love, concern for others, repentance, forgiveness. I have to reflect these in my own life, in my relationships with other people and in relation to the rest of Creation.

Opinions of Muslims on the five pillars. Statements 3, 5 and 6 are adapted from interviews in *What Muslims believe*, edited by John Bowker. The others are from interviews gathered by the authors of this book.

Good intention

NIYYAH means 'intention'. A Muslim's reason for acting can be just as important as the action itself. If a Muslim prays to impress other people, this is not a good or honourable thing to do. So, before all acts of worship such as salah, hajj or sawm, Muslims must state their intention to please Allah.

Any other action done with the intention of pleasing Allah (as long as it is not specifically forbidden within Islam) is also called ibadah, since to please Allah is an act of worship.

Halal and haram

Within Islam there are categories of behaviour. HARAM means 'behaviour which is forbidden'. HALAL means 'behaviour which is permitted'. There are different levels of this. This table summarises the different categories of behaviour.

Category		Definition	Example	Explanation
Halal (permitted)	FARD	Actions that **have to be done**	Salah	Prayer reminds every Muslim of their relationship to Allah.
	MANDUB	Actions that are **recommended**	Helping other people	Allah wants people to be kind to each other.
	MUBAH	Actions that **may be done**	Watching a wildlife programme on television	It does no harm, but brings no benefits either.
	MAKRUH	Actions that are **disapproved of**, although not forbidden	Divorce	Islam is a pragmatic religion, and recognises that not every marriage will succeed.
Haram (forbidden)		Actions that are **forbidden**	Drinking alcohol	Losing control can lead to many harmful consequences

1 Look back at the definitions of absolute and relative approaches to moral decision-making on page 10. Explain whether the following approaches are absolute or relative:
a) judging an action by a person's niyyah (intention)
b) judging an action by whether it is halal (permitted) or haram (forbidden).

ACTIVITY A

Your values might be the same as, similar to or different from those of Islam.

1 Imagine you had to say what was permitted or forbidden according to *your own values*. Work in pairs to agree one everyday action that you would put in each of the five categories:

- have to be done
- recommended
- may be done
- disapproved of
- forbidden.

Make sure you explain why you put it in this category.
2 Where would you put the following:
a) buying a lottery ticket
b) having a tattoo
c) smoking
d) fishing
e) playing truant?
3 Discuss your decisions as a class.

SAVE AS ...

4 Make your own large copy of the chart above, leaving the example and explanation columns blank. As you work through this course add examples of behaviour in each category, and your own explanation of why Muslims regard that behaviour in the way they do.

What would you do if … ?

There are many Muslims in Britain and the community is growing. However, some aspects of modern life can make it difficult for Muslims to practise their faith. The cartoons below show some real dilemmas faced by people interviewed for this book.

Dilemma 1: Too rich?

The time for giving zakah is approaching. I have just received my bank statement and realised that I have saved a lot more money than usual this year. Should I quickly spend some of my savings or pay more zakah?

Dilemma 2: Unpaid leave

I want to ask for unpaid leave to go on Hajj, but I am not sure that my manager will be sympathetic. My colleague who went last year told the manager that she had to go to a funeral overseas. What should I do?

Dilemma 3: Business lunch

I work for a European company. The managing director is coming to Britain during Ramadan to evaluate a project I have been leading. He has suggested that we go out for lunch together to discuss the work. What should I do?

ACTIVITY B

1 What do you think the people who faced the three dilemmas above actually did?
2 Explain why you think they took this course of action.
3 With a partner, think of other dilemmas that a Muslim in Britain today might face. Copy and complete the chart below.

Dilemma or issue	Possible solution

FOCUS TASK

Islam is …

1 Using all that you have so far found out about Islam, complete the statement 'Islam is …' in as many different ways as you can. Each statement should express an important belief or practice of Islam. For example, 'Islam is … believing in one God, Allah'. Write each statement on a separate piece of card.
2 Choose three statements that you think are really important and use them to help you make an 'Islam is …' poster, introducing Islam to people who know nothing about it.

1.4   Who are the Muslims?

Global

A

You can see from Source A that Islam is a global religion. It is followed by one-fifth of the world's population. Today about 15 per cent of all Muslims are Arab, and Muslims are found in at least 120 countries. In half of these, Islam is the majority religion. In many more it is a significant minority. There are 13 million Muslims in China, 45 million in Nigeria, 80 million in India, 165 million in Indonesia.

Percentage of population who are Muslim

	Less than 1%
	1–4%
	5–10%
	11–20%
	21–50%
	51–80%
	81–90%
	91–100%

Diversity

As with all world religions, there is diversity within Islam. Of course, there are features common to Islam everywhere, but the way these are expressed varies from country to country, culture to culture and person to person.

- **Muslims are individuals** with their own cultures and interests and attitudes. These all affect the way they live their faith. They have different levels of personal commitment. They are at different points on their spiritual journey.
- **The freedom Muslims have to implement Shari'ah varies**. In some countries Islam is the majority religion and the laws try to build on Islamic principles; Islamic attitudes and practices are part of the very fabric of society; being a Muslim is part of the national identity. In other countries, in Britain for example, Muslims are in a minority. The application of Islam in such countries is very different.
- **Traditions vary.** The two main traditions within Islam are called Sunni and Shi'ah (see Checkpoint). Sometimes they have different views on issues.

With such diversity, it is impossible for this course to capture all the varied colours of Islam in today's world. So we have chosen to focus particularly on the dynamics of Islam in Britain today.

- There are about 1.5 million Muslims in Britain. They come from many racial groups. The map of Britain on this page previews some of the people who feature in case studies in this book.
- Throughout this book we have tried to focus on committed, faithful Muslims – those who sincerely believe in the faith they declare in the Shahadah, who sincerely attempt to follow the moral code of Islam including the Five Pillars, who have a sincere belief in Allah the Judge and the Creator.

The global distribution of Islam

✓ CHECKPOINT

Sunni and Shi'ah

These are the two main branches of Islam: SUNNI Muslims represent about 90 per cent of the world's Muslim population and SHI'AH Muslims about 10 per cent. Sunni and Shi'ah Muslims agree on most aspects of Islam. However, they have some different ideas about sources of authority and the succession of Muhammad 鎌.

When Muhammad 鎌 died the community agreed to continue to follow the teachings of the Qur'an. They did not agree, however, about who should now lead the Muslims.

Some thought ABU BAKR, Muhammad's 鎌 friend and father-in-law, should be the KHALIFAH (successor). Others favoured ALI, Muhammad's 鎌 cousin and son-in-law.

Abu Bakr was chosen. When he died he was followed by UMAR, and after him UTHMAN. Finally, 24 years after Muhammad's 鎌 death, Ali became Khalifah.

Sunni Muslims call these four the 'Rightly Guided Khalifahs'. They had all lived and worked with Muhammad 鎌 personally, so their decisions could be followed as if they had been made by Muhammad 鎌 himself.

Shi'ah Muslims believe that Ali should have succeeded Muhammad 鎌 directly and do not accept the authority of the three preceding Khalifahs.

This affects the ideas about authority and leadership that the two groups hold to this day.

Sunni Muslims accept the Hadith based on the sayings and stories transmitted by the four Rightly Guided Khalifahs. They do not believe that some individuals are Allah's special representatives. For them, authority ends with the Qur'an and Muhammad 鎌. All people are created equal and every Muslim has a direct relationship with Allah through prayer and careful reading of the Qur'an.

So, when a situation arises that requires a moral decision, Sunni Muslims consult people who are knowledgeable about the Qur'an and Hadith and Shari'ah. These people consult with each other and make a decision collectively. The whole Sunni community should then follow what the majority have decided is best. For example, in 1995, a group of 18 knowledgeable British Muslims issued a FATWA (legal guidance based on the Qur'an, Sunnah and Shari'ah) declaring that organ transplants were allowable under Shari'ah.

Shi'ah Muslims believe that Ali was much more than the fourth in a series of Khalifahs – he was the first of twelve Imams (not to be confused with the Sunni imam) who spoke with special authority. For Shi'ah Muslims, Imams must be descended from Muhammad 鎌 through Ali and his wife FATIMAH AL-ZAHRAH (Muhammad's 鎌 youngest daughter). These Imams had a special gift, sometimes called a 'guiding light', which other Muslims do not have. They could interpret Allah's words (the Qur'an) and use that knowledge to make laws (Shari'ah) to guide people in their moral decision-making. Shi'ah Muslims believe that because Allah was guiding them, the Imams had no faults and made no mistakes. Most Shi'ah Muslims also believe that the twelfth Imam will return again as the Messiah, called AL-MAHDI, which means 'the Rightly Guided one who is awaited.'

In the absence of the Imam, a Shi'ah Muslim follows a single scholar whom he/she regards as his/her representative, called a MARJ'AH. The majority of Shi'ah Muslims in the UK regard Syed Ali Sistani, who lives in Najaf in Iraq, as their Marj'ah. When a new situation arises, the Marj'anah issue a fatwa to guide Shi'ah Muslims.

1.5 How can individual Muslims change the world around them?

A

> ... a Muslim social worker highlighted the physical, mental and emotional abuse many Muslim women were suffering. More shocking was that no Muslim help was available for Muslim women in the UK who were suffering oppression, violence and cruelty – often in the name of a religion which was supposed to have liberated them.
>
> In the women's restroom, I was met by women talking about the session they had just attended.
>
> 'Sarah,' one of them said, 'We must do something. We can't just walk away as if nothing happened. Will you come to a meeting to discuss a helpline for Muslim women?'

Sarah Sheriff

---

1 **List all the methods used by the Helpline counsellors in the cases in Source B.**
2 **Why is the growing use of the Helpline both good news and bad news?**
3 **What is distinctively Muslim about the help offered? Explain your answer carefully with reference to sources D and E.**

The word 'JIHAD' is used in the Qur'an to describe the challenge of doing what is right and good. It literally means every Muslim's individual struggle to resist the NAFS (the selfishness that is within everyone) in order to follow the path of Allah. Most Muslims say that following this path is a positive and exciting challenge and they believe that obedience to Allah – doing what is right and good – will make each person feel at peace in their mind and heart. This in turn will bring peace to the whole of society. In this book you will come across many examples of Muslims who try to change the world around them for the better.

Case study 1: The Muslim Women's Helpline

In 1987 Sarah Sheriff attended a conference for women at London's Central Mosque. She was shocked (see Source A).

The Qur'an and Hadith repeatedly urge Muslims to help others. It is a form of ibadah (worship). It pleases Allah. Muslims have a particular responsibility to help other Muslims, who are all members of the UMMAH, the worldwide community of Muslims (see pages 66–71).

Sarah felt that Muslim women needed help from other Muslim women. That was the only way that appropriate support could be given, as non-Muslim agencies often misunderstood the needs of Muslim women.

A few months after this, Sarah Sheriff met with other concerned women and the Muslim Women's Helpline was launched.

Why do the callers call?

Source B gives details of some of the callers who phoned the Helpline. Most calls deal with marriage or family problems. The Helpline wants to encourage more teenage girls to contact it for help.

B

Reason for calling	Action taken
Tasleema phoned from the 10th floor of a tower block. She had become depressed and isolated since the death of her husband and was addicted to anti-depressant drugs.	Helpline counsellor 'befriended' Tasleema and helped her gradually to stop taking her drugs. Her depression lifted.
An anxious teenage girl, **Yasmine**, phoned saying she was due to have an abortion in two days' time but was having second thoughts.	Counsellor supported Yasmine's need to decide what to do about her pregnancy. As a result of the call Yasmine felt more positive. She decided to get married and to have the baby.
Jon, a distraught father, phoned to say he had beaten up his wife, mother of their seven children.	Counsellors went to the house immediately. They listened to both sides of the story. The couple both expressed remorse and took measures to stop arguing and put the family first.
Basma phoned from a mental hospital in great distress. She had been brain-damaged in an assault, so her sister had had her put into the hospital. She felt abandoned by her family.	Befriender went to the hospital and found Basma in a very poor state. She promised to visit regularly.

Names have been changed to preserve anonymity. Source: *the 1994 Annual Report of the Helpline.*

C

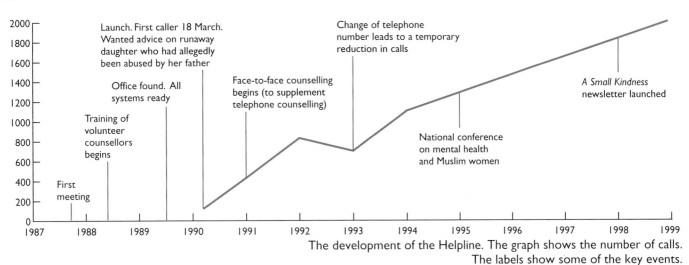

The development of the Helpline. The graph shows the number of calls. The labels show some of the key events.

4 **List all the reasons people give on these two pages for helping the Helpline.**

5 **Look at the Helpline's mission statement in Source D.**
a) Explain what you think it means.
b) Choose one person from Source B and explain how helping that person might 'change a community for the better'.

6 **Most volunteers describe a feeling of responsibility:**
a) to please Allah
b) to help others.
Do you feel that you have responsibilities like this? Explain your answers and say why others may disagree with you.

Why do the helpers help?

The Helpline offers what Sarah Sheriff describes as 'Islamic counselling'. The counsellors believe that Islamic faith is a positive force which unlocks people's potential to grow and to overcome their own problems.

D

Islamic counselling reminds us of Allah's mercy and guidance. It provides a spiritual response to apparently worldly problems. Islamic counselling empowers women to live according to the expectations Allah places upon us . . .

The Helpline has given me the chance, alongside others, to follow one of my favourite maxims: 'Think global, act local.' The Helpline's mission statement is, **'Changing our community for the better – one woman's life at a time.'** This could be seen as a restatement of the instruction in the Qur'an: 'Have faith and do good' – the duty of every one of us.

Sarah Sheriff

The title of the Helpline newsletter, *A Small Kindness* (*ASK* for short), is inspired by the Qur'an. In surah 107 worshippers who begrudge giving even small kindnesses are condemned. The Helpline has been dependent for its survival on the small kindnesses of many ordinary Muslims giving their time and money to keep it going.

E

Women are highly valued in Islam and it is our duty as a community to ensure that this position is maintained.
It is also to seek the rewards from Allah for helping others.

N. Sibassi, father of two

I spent the last ten years bringing up two children single-handed, juggling work with running a home. Ten years on, I thank Allah every single day for the support and strength He has given me. But feeling grateful is no longer enough; the strong woman I am today can help another woman. Joining the Helpline is my humble way of thanking Him.

B. Kharoubi

In 1997 *A Small Kindness* asked some of the Helpline's committee members why they helped.

Case study 2: Farid Esack and the Call of Islam

Most people would agree that helping others is a good thing. But what if helping others means getting involved in controversy? This was the case for South African Muslim, Farid Esack.

Farid is senior lecturer in Religious Studies at the University of the Western Cape in South Africa. Throughout his life he has struggled to combine his faith in the teachings of Islam with his fight against racism and inequality in South Africa. After much discussion with people of other religions, and reflection on his own Muslim faith, he has developed a controversial Islamic 'LIBERATION THEOLOGY'. He believes that Muslims should be involved in political action on the side of the poor, that they should challenge injustice wherever they see the laws of Allah being broken, and that they should work with people of other religions to change society for the better. Islam teaches Muslims to obey those in authority, but not when doing so would cause them to disobey the greater authority of Allah (see Checkpoint on page 22).

FARID ESACK CAMPAIGNER FOR FREEDOM

1   *Farid Esack's childhood was a struggle with poverty.*

My father left my mother when I was three weeks old. My mother was left to bring up six sons on her own.

2   *As a 'mixed-race' Asian South African, he was treated as a 'second-class citizen' in racially segregated South Africa. When he was five years old his family were forced to move into a township for 'coloured' people in the Cape Province. They had to beg or scavenge on rubbish dumps for food.*

3   *Even at an early age, his Muslim religion was very important to Farid. With seven people crammed into a two-bedroomed house, Farid would find any space he could to make his daily prayers.*

4   *At the age of nine he joined the 'Tablighi Jama'ah', a movement that calls door-to-door to invite people to come to the mosque.*

5   *At the same time I was campaigning against apartheid, despite the fact that the Tablighi Jama'ah is completely opposed to political activity.*

6   *While still at school, Farid was detained by the police because of his links with a radical students' group called National Youth Action.*

7

> In prison I felt supported by the presence of Allah. I continued to pray regularly.

8 *Farid was in conflict not only with the government but also with other Muslims, who thought he was wrong to get involved in politics.*

> There was not one Farid, but two: one political, one religious. But I wouldn't abandon the liberation struggle in South Africa, nor was I going to abandon my religion. It gave me meaning at the deepest level. I knew too that religion is a powerful weapon. It should be used in favour of the poor.

9 *Farid went to train at a Muslim seminary in Pakistan.*

> In Pakistan I met some Christians who helped me to see the contradictions. I had been taught not to mix religion and politics, but really there was no distinction. If this meant facing opposition, I thought, 'So be it.'
> Religion is far too important to be left in the hands of people remote from the struggles of everyday life, or people who are arrogant enough to think that their beliefs are the only ones that matter. My religion was on the side of the poor.

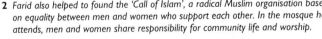

10

> The most excellent jihad (struggle) is the uttering of truth in the presence of an unjust ruler.
> Tirmidhi Hadith 17

11 *Back in South Africa, Farid rejoined the struggle against apartheid, which finally collapsed in 1994. He now works for the new South African state, which is founded on non-racialism and non-sexism. He was the only man appointed by former President Mandela to the Gender Equality Commission, a state body working to rebuild South African society after the apartheid era.*

12 *Farid also helped to found the 'Call of Islam', a radical Muslim organisation based on equality between men and women who support each other. In the mosque he attends, men and women share responsibility for community life and worship.*

13 *Farid Esack questions the way the world is headed.*

> If I look at the direction the world is headed, uncontrolled industrialisation and so on, I see only two ways out – the complete destruction of humankind or finding more humane ways of conducting our business here on Earth, where people work together in a caring way, planning for the long-term future of the planet. In this way, people could use the world's resources effectively to bring about equality, regardless of religion, gender or ethnicity. And I am not alone in this. Many others – whatever their religion – are realising the need for change.

✓ CHECKPOINT

The individual in society

For your exam, you will need to consider how their religion affects the way Muslims view authority and serve others.

Islam and authority

One meaning of the word 'Islam' is 'peace', and Muslims try to lead peaceful lives.

Islam teaches them to behave as responsible citizens wherever they live. They should respect a country's laws and obey its orders. Muslims who do not accept a state's laws should leave rather than enter into conflict.

On pages 20–21 you studied the situation of Farid Esack in South Africa. Under the apartheid government, black people and 'coloured' people, many of whom were Muslim, were treated unfairly. They were in personal danger if they tried to complain publicly about their treatment. What should a Muslim do in such a situation? They could not leave the country. In extreme cases, where political leaders openly disregard the authority of Allah, Islam allows the authority of the head of state to be challenged. Two hadith are particularly relevant to Muslim attitudes to political authority.

F

The most excellent jihad is the uttering of truth in the presence of an unjust ruler.

Tirmidhi Hadith 17

The Prophet ﷺ invited us so we swore allegiance to him; and among the conditions which he laid down on us to follow was this: that he had a promise from us to hear and obey, whether we liked or disliked an order, and whether we were in adversity or ease, even if our rights were not granted; and that we should not dispute the authority of those entrusted with it, adding, 'Unless you see an act of open disbelief in which you have a clear argument from Allah.'

Bukhari Hadith 93.2

Service to others

Service to others is a form of ibadah – an act done to please Allah. The Qur'an and Hadith repeatedly encourage Muslims to help other people. Muhammad ﷺ provided a clear example to follow in this respect.

All Muslims who can afford to give zakah (see page 98) for the welfare of the poor. Muslims should also give SADAQAH, a voluntary payment or good deed for charitable purposes. Most Muslims feel themselves to be part of the ummah, the Muslim community (see page 67), and to have a particular duty to care for and serve other members of that community. On pages 18–19 you studied the motivation of Sarah Sheriff and other members of the Muslim Women's Helpline. They felt a duty to care for other Muslim women. However, many Muslims also feel drawn to caring for non-Muslims of their own nationality.

G

As Muhammad ﷺ said,

'Every good action is a charity and it is a good action to meet a friend with a smiling face.'

Mushad of Ahmad Hadith 6.6

'Sadaqah is the responsibility of every Muslim.'

His companions said, 'O Prophet of Allah. What about a person who has nothing to give?'

He said, 'He should work, earn and give in charity.'

They said, 'If he has nothing in spite of this?'

'He should help a distressed person, one who is in need.'

They said, 'If he is unable to do this?'

He said, 'He should do good deeds and not do bad things, this is charity on his part.'

Bukhari Hadith 24.31

Muhammad ﷺ said,

'Believers are in relation to one another as parts of one structure. One part strengthens the other.'

Bukhari Hadith 8.88

FOCUS TASK

Over the past five pages you have studied different ways in which Muslims might influence the world around them. These different ways are not conflicting. Most people would say that if religious believers are to influence the world around them they need to combine these two approaches: helping individuals who are in need and trying to change injustices in society as well.

1   Work in pairs. You are going to prepare interviews with Farid Esack and Sarah Sheriff to form part of a radio programme called: 'The individual in society'. Think about what each of them might say about:
    a) their Muslim motivation in their work, and how they might support that from the Qur'an and Hadith
    b) their methods of helping others

c) how their own methods are similar to or different from that of the other person.
    Record the interviews and then think about what else you are going to include in your radio programme.

2   Explain whether you agree with each of the following statements.
    a) 'Religious believers have a greater responsibility than non-believers to help other people in their community.'
    b) 'Religious believers have a greater responsibility than non-believers to protest against injustice in society.'
    In each case give reasons for your answer showing that you have considered other points of view. Support your answer with examples drawn from Islam and especially from pages 18–22 of this book.

UNIT 2

Thinking about Allah

I bear witness that there is no god except Allah and that Muhammad is the Messenger of Allah

This is the Shahadah. It is sometimes called 'the door to Islam' (see page 13). If someone wants to become a Muslim, they must publicly make this declaration of faith, **and sincerely mean it.** It expresses the two most fundamental beliefs of Islam, about Allah and the role of Muhammad ﷺ.

In this unit you will investigate these beliefs in greater depth. Some ideas might be new to you. Others might be familiar. Some beliefs you might share. Others you might disagree with. Whatever your beliefs, this unit aims to help you understand what Muslims believe about Allah, to compare these beliefs with your own and to help you express your own views clearly and convincingly.

For Muslims, belief and practice are not separated. As you saw on page 4, Muslims see Islam as a way of life directing all their attitudes, their habits and their beliefs. So the beliefs you look at in this section will be all-important. They will help you understand the Muslim responses to moral issues which you will study later in the course.

2.1 The One and Only ...

Imagine an ant with a broken leg setting out to walk the 200 miles across the desert from Makkah to MADINAH. The Muslim spiritual leader Sheikh Nazim Al-Haqqani describes the process of trying to understand Allah as being like this. The ant will not succeed but still it tries. Nor will any human mind ever succeed in understanding Allah, but still Muslims try. And ... (this is the point) it is worth Muslims trying, even if they only catch a small glimpse of some of the truth about Allah.

Tawhid = oneness or unity

Source A is one of the best known surahs of the Qur'an. Most Muslims learn this surah by heart, just as they learn Al-Fatihah (see pages 1–2). Around the surah you can see the notes that this translator has made. You can see from his notes that each time a Muslim recites these four well-known verses, many important meanings are expressed.

Most of all, this surah summarises the belief in TAWHID. Tawhid means 'the Oneness or Unity of Allah'. Allah is **the one and only, universal God of all humanity**. He is all-powerful, transcendent, beyond anything human beings can ever imagine.

FOCUS TASK

1 **Read Source A carefully. Try to connect each of notes 2–8 with one word or line of the surah.**
2 **On a large sheet of paper, draw a diagram like this one:**

Allah

3 **Start your diagram by adding the ideas about Allah mentioned in Source A. Put them into your own words where possible.**
4 **Add any other ideas about Allah that you have read about earlier in this book. Look in particular at Al-Fatihah on pages 1–2.**
5 **Keep your diagram and add to it as you work through this unit.**

A

1 The qualities of Allah are described in many places elsewhere. Here we are especially taught to avoid the common mistakes in trying to understand Allah.

2 His nature is so far beyond our limited minds that the best we can do is to feel He is a Personality, not an abstract concept. He is near us; He cares for us; we owe our existence to Him.

3 He is the only One to worship; all other things or beings we can think of are His creation and in no way comparable to Him.

4 This verse is to oppose the idea of polytheism (belief in many gods).

5 He is without beginning or end.

6 He is not limited by time or place or circumstance.

7 This is to oppose the Christian idea of 'the Father', 'the only-begotten Son', etc.

8 This sums up the whole argument and warns us especially against anthropomorphism, the tendency to describe Allah in human terms, a tendency that creeps in at all times and among all peoples.

Say:

He is Allah,

The One and Only;

Allah, the Eternal, Absolute;

He begot none,

Nor was He begotten;

And there is none like Him.

Surah 112.1–4, called Al-Ikhlas (Purity of Faith). The notes around it are adapted from notes made by the translator Yusuf Ali.

How does belief in Tawhid affect a Muslim's life?

- A MONOTHEIST believes in one God. Islam is a monotheistic religion
- A POLYTHEIST believes in more than one god. Islam is strongly opposed to polytheism.

In the time of Muhammad ﷺ, Makkah was a centre for polytheism. People came from miles around to worship hundreds of idols and images which were kept in and around the KA'BAH. These idols were made out of stone, wood or even food, and people would consult them about all sorts of things, such as who to marry, how to settle arguments or which was the safest route for a journey. They believed the idols had power to affect their lives. The traders of Makkah made lots of money from the visitors.

Muhammad ﷺ brought the same message as had been sent through earlier prophets (see pages 32–3): that people should worship the one true God, Allah.

The call of Islam was for the people of Makkah to abandon idol-worship, and for Jews and Christians to return to the true origins of their faith in the one true God.

In 630CE Muhammad ﷺ removed the idols from the Ka'bah, and re-established it as a place for the worship of Allah alone. To this day Muslims all over the world pray facing the Ka'bah, the symbol of monotheism.

When Muslims say 'God is One', they are declaring their monotheism. They are also declaring all that follows from it.

If there is **One God –**	greater than anything we could ever imagine
there is **One universe –**	created by Allah, ordered and arranged by Allah, which despite its unimaginable, massive scale is still much less than Allah
One will that rules the universe –	and only one will. If there was more than one God, each with an independent will, there would be chaos
One Earth –	created by Allah. There is a purpose to Allah's creation, and a purpose for the presence of the human race on Earth
One humanity –	whose members are all equal before Allah, with no barriers of gender or race or religion to divide from one another. There is not 'my God' and 'your God', there is one God: our God
One basic aim for humanity –	to worship the One God and resist the worship of false gods
One message to humanity –	all prophets who bring the message of One God are brothers
One plan –	a plan for every person's life all people are part of Allah's plan and live their lives accordingly

Muslims believe that there is one being, Allah, who gave them life and made them the person they are. As they look around them at the wonders of the universe they again see the work of this one being. They believe that this one being sees all that they do and that after death the same one being will judge them.

You can see that Tawhid is a big idea. It is an almost all-embracing concept.

In the face of Tawhid, an individual must be in awe, overwhelmed, obedient, full of respect for the one all-powerful, all-knowing, transcendent Allah who sees and judges every move.

The only acceptable response is to submit. The word Islam means **submission to Allah.** A Muslim is one who submits to Allah. A belief in Tawhid should result in submission by all individuals whatever their status; from street cleaners to presidents. All should submit to the higher authority of Allah.

That is the concept, and for many Muslims it is also the practice. However, submission to Allah's authority is not easy for all human beings, even when they believe that the authority is right. So very few Muslims can live up to this ideal all the time. Even Muhammad ﷺ himself used to weep for his shortcomings.

SAVE AS …

For your exam you might need to know how belief in Tawhid affects a Muslim's life. The examiners are looking not only for your understanding of the word Tawhid, but also for some of the depth of meaning that lies behind it. To practise, record your answers to these questions:

1 **What is Tawhid?**
2 **What ideas would a Muslim have in mind when they use the word?**
3 **Here are some good personal qualities which a Muslim might want to develop:**

   bravery   determination   honesty   modesty   obedience   contentedness self-respect   respect for environment.

   Choose three that you think would be most likely to result from a belief in Tawhid and explain your choice.
4 **How might submission to Allah affect the way people, races or countries relate to each other?**

The 'names' of Allah

In the Qur'an and Hadith many different 'names' are used to describe Allah. These are sometimes referred to as 'the ninety-nine names of Allah', although different lists include different names. Many Muslims develop their awareness of Allah by reciting the names as one of the forms of DHIKR (see Checkpoint on page 37). Source B is a Muslim artist's expression of the ninety-nine names. Allah cannot be completely described by any, or even all, of these names, but they may help Muslims to contemplate Allah's unknowable nature.

These names help convey some of Allah's attributes (qualities). Describing any non-human in terms of human qualities is called anthropomorphism. The risk of this anthropomorphism is that people will view Allah as a bigger, better human being. So the Qur'an reminds Muslims that Allah is beyond human understanding.

'No vision can grasp Him, but His grasp is over all vision

He is above all understanding, yet He understands all things.' (Surah 6.103).

B

The attributes of divine perfection by Ahmed Moustafa (1987)

DISCUSS

A Muslim would never draw a picture of Allah because people may be tempted to worship the picture and idolatry is strictly forbidden in the Qur'an. For many centuries Muslim artists have used calligraphy (decorative writing) and other forms of design to express important ideas about Allah. Look at the examples on pages 1, 23, 28, 47 and 65. Usually the artist uses words from the Qur'an and builds these into a pattern.

1 Talk with a partner about your first impressions of Source B. Do you like or dislike it as a piece of art? Why?
2 What does it make you think?
3 How does it make you feel?
4 How effective is it in making you think about Allah?

ACTIVITY

This is a translation of some of the 'names of Allah'. You can get a full list from your teacher.

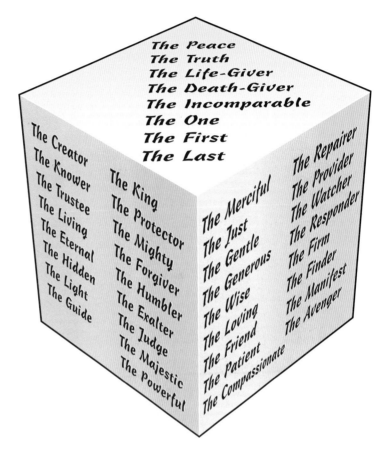

The Peace
The Truth
The Life-Giver
The Death-Giver
The Incomparable
The One
The First
The Last

The Creator
The Knower
The Trustee
The Living
The Eternal
The Hidden
The Light
The Guide

The King
The Protector
The Mighty
The Forgiver
The Humbler
The Exalter
The Judge
The Majestic
The Powerful

The Merciful
The Just
The Gentle
The Generous
The Wise
The Loving
The Friend
The Patient
The Compassionate

The Repairer
The Provider
The Watcher
The Responder
The Firm
The Finder
The Manifest
The Avenger

The range of names encourages a variety of responses. Some invite closeness and intimacy; some respect or awe.
Work in small groups.

1 As a group, take four or five 'names'. Do not take more than one from any column. Write each 'name' on a separate card.
2 Discuss what this 'name' suggests about Allah.
3 For each one complete the sentences, 'Allah is called the ... We think this is because ...'

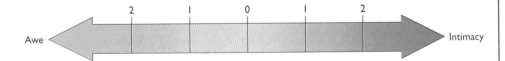

Awe 2 1 0 1 2 Intimacy

4 Draw a line like this. Place your 'names' on this line. At one end put 'names' you associate with intimacy. At the other put 'names' you associate with awe. In the middle put 'names' which seem to combine both.
5 On your own, for each of your 'names' suggest a situation when you think a Muslim might particularly want to think about this quality of Allah. For example, they might think about 'Allah the Forgiver' when they have done something bad. Compare your suggestions with those of others in your group.

✓ CHECKPOINT
Immanent and transcendent

- IMMANENT means 'present in the universe'. To say Allah is immanent is to say Allah is part of human life, can act in human affairs, and can affect daily life.
- TRANSCENDENT means 'outside the created universe', not limited by the rules of nature or time that affect human beings.

The two words are opposites, but Allah is described in both ways in the Qur'an and other Muslim sources, although the emphasis in Islam is always on the transcendence of Allah.

It is a mystery how Allah can be both present and outside, but religious believers are used to many aspects of faith being beyond human understanding.

A Muslim writer called Hujwiri, who lived almost 1000 years ago, suggested that a person's relationship with Allah might have two parts; one part that is close and intimate and the other which is based on respect. A Muslim needs to sense both Allah's transcendence and power, and Allah's closeness. Allah is all-powerful, all-seeing, and a judge. But Allah is also all-loving, forgiving and the source of peace.

Read the Checkpoint.
1 The Qur'an says, 'Wherever you turn there is the face of Allah, and God is all-embracing, all knowing.' (Surah 2.115). Is this a description of Allah as immanent or transcendent?
2 Explain how Sources C and D help convey Allah's immanence or transcendence?

Immanent and transcendent

Islam emphasises the absolute transcendence of Allah (see Checkpoint). However, this does not mean that Allah is remote and unapproachable. The Qur'an and Hadith show that Allah is close to humankind. The descriptions most often used of Allah are 'the Compassionate' and 'the Merciful'. The highest state of Muslim worship, called ihsan (perfection), is to worship Allah as if you saw Him, because even though you do not, He sees you.

C

He is the Omnipotent by Iraqi artist Issam El-Said (1983)

D

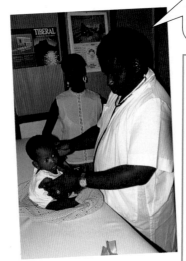

Allah tells us in the Qur'an (Surah 50.16) that He is 'closer to us than our jugular vein.' This is your jugular vein. It runs from the brain to the heart.

FOCUS TASK

W rite an acrostic poem, using one idea about Allah as the
R oot word.
I n an acrostic poem
T he first letter of
E ach line spells out the root word.

1 In your poem, express some of the ideas about Allah that you have studied over the last six pages.
2 You could use an attribute of Allah (from page 27) as your root word. You could use a phrase such as 'The One and Only' or a concept such as 'Tawhid' (see pages 24–5). You can use either an Arabic word or an English word as your root word.
3 Do not worry if your poem is not written in perfect sentences, just allow your ideas to flow.
4 Decorate your poem with a traditional Islamic-style border. You can see an example on pages 84–5.

2.2 How is Allah revealed to human beings?

Types of revelation

There are two types of revelation:

- GENERAL REVELATION is indirect and available to everyone. Some truths about Allah can be revealed through the natural world, through reason, through conscience or moral sense (see below).
- SPECIAL REVELATION is direct revelation to an individual or a group. A special revelation gives insights into the will or nature of Allah that could not have been given by general revelation alone. Something new about Allah might be revealed through, for example, a dream, vision, prophecy or experience. In Islam, the angel Jibril is a channel of revelation from Allah to the Prophets.

Over the next four pages you are going to investigate these ideas in greater depth.

GENERAL REVELATION

Can point people to Allah ...

According to the Qur'an, the natural world points people towards Allah. Allah designed the universe, created it, cares for it and sustains it. From the infinity of space to the intricate workings of the human body, creation is evidence of Allah. All things are created by Allah and are signs of Allah's power and sustaining care. Studying these things can guide the seeker to truth about Allah.

But it isn't enough to show them the whole truth ...

While general revelation points people towards Allah, it is not enough on its own. For example, studying the natural world:

- cannot answer the big questions about humanity and our place in creation
- cannot provide rules for human conduct
- cannot explain the purpose of creation
- cannot tell people anything about the unseen world of the spirits.

For those things, a special revelation from Allah is needed. The Qur'an is this 'special revelation'.

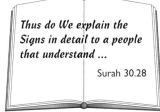

Thus do We explain the Signs in detail to a people that understand ...

Surah 30.28

Fitrah

According to the Qur'an, human beings have a natural tendency to see and worship the Creator. This is called FITRAH. This instinctive need of Allah, this kind of 'built-in' spirituality makes everyone capable of recognising the presence of Allah. It also gives people an instinctive moral sense – an understanding of the distinction between right and wrong.

The natural world

B

Imagine a palace with luxurious furniture, standing on a high mountain in thick forest. Suppose that a man found this house but could not find anybody nearby. Suppose that he thought:

- that rocks from the mountain had collected themselves together to shape this splendid palace with its bedrooms, chambers and corridors;
- that the trees from the forest had split, of their own accord, into boards and formed themselves into doors and beds, seats and tables, each taking its place in the palace;
- that the fibres from the plants and the hair of the animals had, of their own accord, changed into embroidered cloth, carpets, pillows and cushions and dispersed about the rooms and settled onto the sofas and chairs;

> And among His Signs is the creation of the heavens and the Earth ...
>
> Surah 30.22

A

Do they not look
At the sky above them?—
How We have made it
And adorned it,
And there are no
Flaws in it?

And the Earth—
We have spread it out,
And set thereon
    mountains
Standing firm, and
    produced
Therein every kind of
Beautiful growth in
    pairs—

Surah 50.6–7

C

Muslims see God-given order in the patterns of the natural world.

D

I listen with reverence to the birdsong cascading at dawn from the oasis, for it seems to me there is no better evidence for the existence of Allah than in the bird that sings, though it knows not why, from a spring of untrammelled joy that wells up in its heart.

Allah of a Hundred Names by an Arab chieftain

* *that the lamps and chandeliers had fallen from all directions and fixed themselves into the ceilings, singly and in groups;*

would you not conclude that this must be the reasoning of someone disturbed in his mind?

What, then, do you think of a palace whose ceiling is the sky, whose floor is the earth, whose pillars are the mountains, whose decoration is the plants and whose lamps are the stars, moon and sun? Is it not likely to direct the mind to a Shaping Creator, Everlasting, Self-Subsistent, who determined and guided?

Abridged from *The Creed of Islam* by Dr Muhammad Abdullah Draz

ACTIVITY

1 **A person who buys a product such as a new car is often given an evaluation form to fill in. Imagine that you are filling in a form to evaluate the Earth. Do you think it has been well made? What would you like to see improved?**

SAVE AS ...

2 **Either:**
 Do you agree with the writer of Source B that the natural world points people towards Allah? Explain your view, showing that you have considered another point of view.
 Or:
 Do you agree with the writer of Source D that a bird's desire to sing is a sign of Allah's existence? Explain your view, showing that you have considered another point of view.

SPECIAL REVELATION

Prophecy

A key part of Muslim belief is the role of the prophet.

We send the messengers only to give good news and to warn ...

Surah 6.48

What is a prophet?

Prophets are human beings who are chosen to carry guidance from Allah to people. Muslims believe that Allah has sent many prophets throughout history. The Qur'an mentions 25 (see Source E).

All the prophets brought the same message – the call to worship Allah as the one true God.

The earlier revelations from Allah were ignored, changed, lost or forgotten. Muhammad ﷺ was Allah's final prophet, 'the seal of the prophets'. His responsibility was to carry Allah's final revelation: the Qur'an.

The 25 prophets mentioned in the Qur'an. The five main prophets of Islam are known as the 'resolute' ones. They are NUH (Noah), IBRAHIM (Abraham), MUSA (Moses), ISA (Jesus) and Muhammad ﷺ. When a Muslim says the name of any of these prophets, they may add 'Peace be upon him', just as they say 'The blessing of Allah be upon him and peace' after the name of Muhammad ﷺ.

E

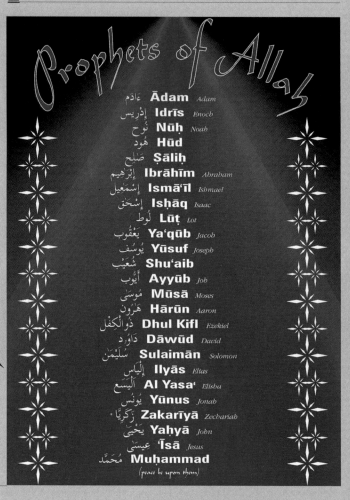

Prophets of Allah

	Ādam	Adam
	Idrīs	Enoch
	Nūḥ	Noah
	Hūd	
	Ṣāliḥ	
	Ibrāhīm	Abraham
	Ismā'īl	Ishmael
	Isḥāq	Isaac
	Lūṭ	Lot
	Ya'qūb	Jacob
	Yūsuf	Joseph
	Shu'aib	
	Ayyūb	Job
	Mūsā	Moses
	Hārūn	Aaron
	Dhul Kifl	Ezekiel
	Dāwūd	David
	Sulaimān	Solomon
	Ilyās	Elias
	Al Yasa'	Elisha
	Yūnus	Jonah
	Zakarīyā	Zechariah
	Yahyā	John
	Īsā	Jesus
	Muhammad	

(peace be upon them)

The Qur'an

Muhammad ﷺ did not write the Qur'an. It was revealed to him (see Checkpoint). Throughout the Qur'an the voice of Allah is speaking.

The Qur'an was revealed in Arabic. Most Muslims learn Arabic so as to be able to speak and hear the words of the Qur'an in the original form.

This is the book; it contains true guidance that is not to be doubted. It will guide those who fear God.

Surah 2.2

1 In your own words explain the difference between general and special revelation. Give examples of each from pages 29–33.

F

It has inspired many and transformed their lives forever,
It is a miracle of purity and wisdom,
It is a Divine source which perfects the very soul,
It contains the most eloquent, beauteous words ever revealed to man.
It has warmed the heart and clothed it in beautiful teachings,
It is unique and no price can be put on its value.
It is the inspiration of all books,
Words alone cannot describe its fineness.
It contains not a shred of doubt,
It is the most magnificent, powerful Book, in all existence,
And will always remain so,
Read the Truth, for it's in the Last Testament,
The Holy Qur'an.

A description of the Qur'an by Rahilla Choudhury, from *Trends*

2 Look up 'resolute' in a dictionary. What do you think Muslims mean when they describe prophets as resolute (Source E?)

How did the prophets get their message?

Muslims believe that however wise the prophets may have been, their message does not come from their own wisdom, but from Allah. It is special revelation. It gives knowledge that wisdom, intelligence or moral sense could never reveal.

These messages were given directly to the prophets by Allah or via Jibril. Because the message comes from Allah, the revelation is accurate.

What did the prophets do with their message?

Each prophet had to convey Allah's message by their words and actions. They must be model human beings. Throughout Muhammad's ﷺ life, the people who lived with him observed his actions and listened to his teaching. His sayings and deeds were gathered together as collections called Hadith (see page 9). These carry great authority in Islam.

What was the message?

All the prophets had as their main task to call people to Tawhid (see page 24).

They also had to tell people about the unseen world, warn people about the Day of Judgement and help people achieve salvation and fight evil.

The special mission of the Prophet Muhammad ﷺ was to perfect and complete this guidance. The last words of the Qur'an to be revealed say, 'Today I have perfected your religion for you, completed my favour upon you and have chosen Islam as your way of life.' (Surah 5.3).

Were prophets special people?

Although the prophets were 'model human beings', they were also ordinary human beings. They ate, slept, married and died. They were often rejected precisely because they were ordinary human beings.

Are there any prophets today?

Muhammad ﷺ was the last of the prophets. There are no prophets today.

✓ CHECKPOINT

The revelation of the Qur'an

In your exam, you might need to know what type of revelation the Qur'an is. The answer is not simple! However, the answer the question will be looking for is that the Qur'an was a special revelation to Muhammad ﷺ. You can see why.

Muslims believe that Muhammad ﷺ received unique insights that could not have been gained through the natural world or through his own wisdom or intelligence, or his common sense. For Muslims, the Qur'an is a miracle for this reason and many others. It says in the Qur'an itself that through it Allah 'teaches man what he does not know.'

How was the Qur'an revealed?

Muhammad ﷺ often spent the whole month of Ramadan in the hills. One year, when Muhammad ﷺ was about 40 years old, he heard a voice speaking to him. It told him to 'Recite.' (Iqra). He saw the angel Jibril who had brought him a message from Allah. It was as if the words were written on his heart. In a second revelation he was told to tell the people of Makkah that there was one God.

For many days Muhammad ﷺ was in a state of shock. When he recovered and returned to Makkah, his wife Khadijah and his family were in no doubt that he had received a message from Allah.

During the next 23 years of his life, Muhammad ﷺ received many more revelations. Each was memorised, and written down in its original form.

The Qur'an as a revelation to others

The Qur'an was given to all people for all time to guide them to worship Allah. The Qur'an is central to the life of all Muslims. Muslims love the Qur'an for its power and beauty. It gives them pleasure to use it in prayer and to memorise it. They refer to it for answers to moral or theological questions. Some Muslims learn the whole Qur'an by heart. Parents teach their children the Qur'an. Muslim schools run classes in the Qur'an; from infancy Muslims are surrounded by the words and ideas of the Qur'an so as they grow up they can act on it almost instinctively.

THE STORY OF YUSUF ISLAM

I wish I could tell, what makes a heaven and what makes a hell.

1 Yusuf Islam grew up in a Christian household in London. His father was Greek and his mother was Swedish. He first came to the attention of the world in the 1960s as the pop singer Cat Stevens. He was rich, talented and famous.

2 He was also living a wild life. Then, when he was only 20 years old, he was diagnosed with tuberculosis. During his two-year convalescence he began to evaluate his life. His songs at this time were full of questions about life and its purpose.

3 Back on the road, life was too busy for these questions. His record sales boomed. Then in 1977 his life took a dramatic turn. While staying at the seaside house of his record company boss, Jerry Moss, in Malibu in the west of the USA he got into difficulties swimming. A strong current was pulling him out to sea. He tried to swim back but the current pulled him further out.

5

Oh God, if you save me, I'll work for you.

Did God really do that?

4 He called out to God. Suddenly he found that the sea was pushing him back to the shore.

I will serve Allah and submit to Allah's will.

I bear witness that there is no god except Allah . . .

7 After a year and a half studying the Qur'an and meeting Muslims, he made his declaration of faith at the Central London Mosque in Regent's Park. He changed his name to Yusuf Islam. Yusuf is the name of a prophet and means 'Allah will increase'.

6 His elder brother David gave him a copy of the Qur'an. For many years Cat had been the centre of his own universe: wealthy and powerful, in control. But in the Qur'an he read that the meaning of the word 'Islam' is 'submission'. It seemed that the purpose of his life was to serve Allah. His own success counted for little. He was part of a much bigger plan, the plan of Allah. This message swept through his life like a breath of fresh air …

1 **Explain the role of these forms of revelation in the story of Yusuf Islam:**
  a) fitrah (see page 29)
  b) experience
  c) the Qur'an.

8 Yusuf Islam has become a leading figure in the Muslim community in Britain. He has founded an Islamic school in north London. He is active in four charities involved in relief work (see page 100 for example). He brought four hostages back from Iraq at the height of the Gulf War. He has set up his own company, Mountain of Light Productions, to spread the message of Islam to as wide an audience as possible. In 1995 he released a new CD called 'the life of the last prophet'.

✓ CHECKPOINT

Conversion and reversion

'Conversion' is the name often given to the experience of deciding to follow a religion. However, Muslims prefer to use the term 'reversion'.

Muslims believe that everyone is born in a state of fitrah – with an instinct to submit to Allah. They are therefore born Muslim. Islam is 'the natural way' for all people to live. Only their upbringing makes a child follow another faith or none at all.

So when someone decides to follow Islam they are simply reverting (coming back) to the faith they were born into. Many reverts to Islam describe a sense of coming home at the time they decided to follow Islam.

FOCUS TASK

1 **Write a brief account of the incident at Malibu from the standpoint of one of the following:**
  a) a writer for a Muslim newspaper who argues that Allah saved Yusuf Islam's life;
  b) a writer for a secular music magazine who does not believe a miracle occurred, and feels that the music world has lost a great performer.
2 **Get together with a partner who has written from the opposite point of view. Read their account. Are you convinced?**
3 **Either:**
  'Yusuf Islam must have already believed in God when he called out to God to save him. It wasn't the experience that made him believe in God.' Do you agree with this statement? Why might someone else disagree?
  Or:
  'The fact that people have religious experiences like Yusuf Islam's proves that Allah exists.' Do you agree? Explain your view showing that you have thought about another point of view.

ICT ACTIVITY

Research the story of a convert/revert to Islam. You could find information on the Internet. Your teacher can give you a sheet to guide you.

G

> Come to prayer.
> Come to success.
> God is Most Great.

1 **What features of salah might help a Muslim to develop:**
   a) **self-discipline**
   b) **a sense of peace**
   c) **community spirit**
   d) **thankfulness**
   e) **humility**
   f) **taqwa (consciousness of Allah)?**
2 **What do you think are the advantages and disadvantages of salah being compulsory?**
3 **Write three dos and three don'ts for a Muslim to make sure they perform salah properly. Use Sources H–K to help you, but include your own ideas.**

I

A man came to the Prophet and said, 'I cannot pray five times a day.'
'Well then, pray three times,' replied the Prophet.
We were surprised at him saying this and asked him to explain.
'If he prays three times, he will soon want to pray five times,' he said.

Hadith

How does prayer help Muslims to know Allah?

In Source G a MUEZZIN (MU'ADHDHIN in Arabic) is calling Muslims to prayer. Muslims are expected to pray at five set times every day. These prayers are called salah. Salah is one of the five pillars of Islam. It is an essential part of worship. Source H shows the essential elements of salah and WUDU (ritual washing that prepares the Muslim for salah).

Where?

Salah can be made in any clean place. The person praying faces QIBLAH (the direction of the Ka'bah in Makkah). A Muslim can pray on their own, but according to one hadith there is greater reward when the prayers are said with others. Most Muslims gather with others at a mosque for the JUMU'AH prayers, (weekly communal salah shortly after midday on Fridays).

How?

Source H shows the set words and actions. People must dress modestly to pray. The prayers are in simple Arabic, and they are not hard to memorise. The use of the same common language for prayer around the world helps unite Muslims.

H

Muslims say:

> In the name of Allah, the Most Merciful, the Most Kind.

WUDU They wash both hands, up to the wrist.

They rinse their mouth three times.

They wash each arm three times.

They pass wet hands backwards from the forehead to the neck.

They clean their ears and behind their ears.

They clean the back of their neck.

They wash their feet.

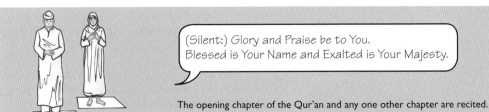

> (Silent:) Glory and Praise be to You. Blessed is Your Name and Exalted is Your Majesty.

The opening chapter of the Qur'an and any one other chapter are recited.

They bow down twice repeating:

> Allah is the Greatest. (Silent:) Glory be to my Lord, the Most High.

> Allah is the Greatest. (Silent:) My Lord, forgive me.

They bow down twice repeating:

> Allah is the Greatest. (Silent:) Glory be to my Lord, the Most High.

Other forms of prayer and meditation

DU'A are personal prayers. Du'a is the Arabic word for 'calling upon'. There are du'a in the Qur'an and in the Hadith. These are often learnt by heart and used. Muslims also make spontaneous du'a.

Dhikr is remembering Allah. It involves reciting the names of Allah or certain phrases from the Qur'an over and over again. Some Muslims use SUBHA (prayer beads) to help them pray dhikr. The beads help them to keep count of the prayers. Dhikr can be done individually or, especially among SUFIS (see page 38), in groups.

Why?

Islam teaches that people have a natural God-given desire to worship. Prayer is the most direct way of communicating with Allah. Through prayer the Muslim develops their personal relationship with Allah and their consciousness of Allah – called 'TAQWA'.

Whether they have been faithful in praying is the first thing a Muslim will be asked on the Day of Judgement (see page 52). Anyone who has sincerely kept the prayers is promised paradise.

When?

Muslims pray five times a day at fixed times.

SAVE AS ...

Complete a table like the one below to summarise the main features of salah. For the third column you will need to use Sources I–K.

Question	Answer	Reason why
Who prays?		
When?		
Where?		
How?		

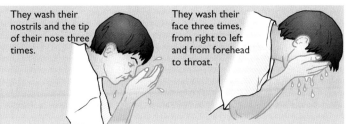

They wash their nostrils and the tip of their nose three times.

They wash their face three times, from right to left and from forehead to throat.

SALAH

I bear witness that there is no god but Allah and that Muhammad is the Messenger of Allah.

Allahu Akbar. (Allah is the Greatest.)

Facing qiblah, each Muslim says how many units of salah (prayer) they intend saying.

Allah is the Greatest. (Silent:) Glory be to my Great Lord and Praise be to Him.

Allah hears those who praise him. Our Lord, All Praise be to you.

Allah is the Greatest.

(Silent:) I bear witness that there is no god but Allah. I bear witness that Muhammad is His Servant and Messenger.

Finally they pray for the Prophet and for peace.

I

The postures of salah show man's relation to his creator – uprightness, reverence, submission and gratitude.

The timing: In the middle of your daily activities salah is a regular reminder of your relationship with Allah, your place in the scheme of things, your responsibilities and your ultimate goal.

Protection: Salah keeps your moral sense sharp. 'Prayer keeps you away from indecency and evil.' (Surah 29.45).

Salah purifies: Washing before the prayer with fresh water acts as a refresher and cleanser. Salah itself, properly performed, purifies the soul.

Salah leads to success in this world or the next. This is the meaning of the resounding 'Come to prayer. Come to success' in the call to prayer. Salah brings mental satisfaction and emotional fulfilment.

Dangers: Despite this, salah can become merely a series of motions and phrases in which the heart and mind are not present. You should guard against this by spending more time preparing for salah.

From *Islam the Natural Way – a guide to Islam*, written for Muslims, by Abdul Wahid Hamid

K

Woe to the praying ones who are unmindful of their prayers, who pray to be seen, and who withhold alms [charity].

Surah 107.4–7

Naphisa Jallo

Naphisa Jallo is a British Muslim who was born in the Gambia, West Africa. She is a Sufi.

L

What's a Sufi?

As a Sufi I try to give up materialistic life for the sake of Allah; to be content with what I have; to spend most of my time worshipping and trying to please Allah.

Wouldn't all Muslims say they try to do that?

Of course. Sufism is still Islam.

So what is different about your way?

We see life as steps to climb.

You reach the middle and you have to decide, 'Do I stay here where most people stay?' I mean, at this stage you know what you should be doing, and you try to do it, but sometimes you fail even though you know you will be punished for bad things and rewarded for good. The point is, at this stage you still have to think. A Sufi tries to climb up to the point where the right way comes automatically. It is about trying to find your inner soul, your inner being, to find peace, and you can't find peace if you are having a debate inside you. Sufis seem a lot happier within themselves than the ordinary person, and a lot more free. They tend not to make a fuss about what they haven't got, or when things go wrong.

How do you achieve that?

By immersing myself in prayer and worship. I begin at 4 a.m. with prayers. I have to begin early to complete 13 cycles of prayer. Then I read the Qur'an. I really find guidance there. I read all 114 surahs at least every two months. Then I perform Dhikr. On a typical morning I might say Shahadah 1000 times and 360 blessings for the Prophet. I keep count with a subha. Then I go to work! I'm a trainee teacher. I fast every Monday and Thursday and the 13th, 14th and 15th day of every month. Most Sufis go regularly to a Sufi Sheikh for guidance; he is an important part of their life.

So have you arrived?

No! Being a Sufi is about struggle with your inner self to find the true way: Al Haqq – the Truth.

Lord Ahmed

Lord Ahmed of Rotherham was appointed to the House of Lords as a Labour member in 1998. He is a Pakistani Muslim who is a successful businessman as well as a magistrate, a councillor and campaigner against racism.

M

Very early on I learnt to read the Qur'an, and my mother used to teach me the Qur'an even when I was a baby. She'd be sewing and I would be sleeping on her lap and she'd be reciting the Qur'an to me. When I was young, the Muslim community in Rotherham started school assembly for the Muslim children. We used to get up at 6 a.m., go to the mosque, read the Qur'an, read the prayers, then go to school and then after school go back again to learn the Qur'an off by heart.

Religion has always been a big part of my life. If I've done anything wrong, I run straight to the mosque and I ask for forgiveness. I've been on Hajj five or six times, and you should see me when I'm holding the door of the Ka'bah. I stand there and I confess and I cry to God because I remember everything that I've done that I think I shouldn't have done, but I do try not to do things that are against Islam.

I went to Makkah three weeks ago to say thank you to God for what He has done for me. What I am today is because of Him, and I went to say thanks to God, in His house, in His place, where I have worshipped before, to say thank you for everything He has given me.

FOCUS TASK

You can see from the case studies on page 38 that each Muslim develops their relationship with **Allah** in a unique way. There is no single set pattern. However, there are common features, and over the last ten pages you have examined the main ways that:
a) revelation, and b) personal experience
help Muslims to develop that relationship.

On page 2 a young Muslim woman called **Nilufa** described the aims of her company, **Al-Fatihah Educational Aids**. She runs courses for Muslim parents. Imagine that you are helping **Nilufa** plan a course.

On your own copy of this table, write summary notes for the middle column explaining how this aspect of revelation develops a person's faith. The page references tell you where in this book you should look. Try to use and explain the key words in the third column.

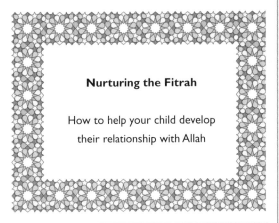

Nurturing the Fitrah

How to help your child develop their relationship with Allah

Idea	How does this help Muslims to know Allah	Key words
The signs of Allah in the natural world	pages 29–31	Creating, Sustaining
The role of the Qur'an	page 33	Comforting, Guiding, Warning
How Allah makes Himself known through Muhammad ﷺ and the Hadith	page 32	Communicating, Exemplifying (being an example)
How religious experience can lead a person to Allah	pages 34–5	Living, Personal
The value of salah and other acts of ibadah e.g. sawm, Hajj, zakah	pages 12–13, 36–8	Closeness, Submitting, Obeying

DISCUSS

1 What does the humorous story in **Source N** tell you about religious experience?
2 Why is it hard to tell whether someone else's religious experience is real or illusory?

N

While Hodja was preaching in the mosque he saw a new face in the crowd below the podium. He noticed that the man was deeply moved. As the sermon progressed the man pulled out a rag and started wiping the tears from his eyes.

Hodja became more and more excited, and at the end of the sermon he asked the frightened man what had moved him so deeply.

'O wise man,' he said. 'I am a goatherd. Last week my best billy-goat died. The more I watched you talk, with your beard dangling, the more I thought of my billy-goat and the sadder I became.'

Hodja is a popular character who appears in hundreds of humorous stories in magazines and books around the Muslim world. He appears under different names. Sometimes the same stories are told about a character called Nazruddin. There is another story about Hodja on page 42.

2.3   Why is suffering part of Allah's plan?

A

ACTIVITY

Work in groups.

1   Discuss what you can see happening in Source A. Explain the link between each scene and the magnified 'problem' threatening it.

2   There are different categories of suffering.

   • **NATURAL SUFFERING** is caused by events beyond human control.

   • **HUMAN-MADE SUFFERING** is caused by human actions.

   Decide whether each problem in Source A is natural suffering or human-made suffering.

3   For each example of human-made suffering decide which of the following was most to blame:
   a) human cruelty
   b) human negligence (ignoring problems)
   c) human greed.

4   Some types of suffering are hard to categorise. Here are some more examples. Are they natural, human-made, or a combination?

   a) A woman with a birthmark covering half her face dares not leave her house. People stare at her and she cannot bear it.

   b) A party of skiers dies in an avalanche triggered when one of them tries to do some daring off-piste skiing.

   c) A life-long smoker dies of lung cancer.

   d) A teenager is so anxious about her figure that she suffers from anorexia.

   e) A whole family is killed when their house collapses in an earthquake.

   f) A whole family is killed when their house is destroyed by a bomb.

SAVE AS ...

5   Write a short story about one example of human-made suffering. Show the causes and consequences of the suffering. Make sure your story shows how human greed, human negligence or human cruelty contributed to the problem.

How does Islam explain suffering?

For some people the existence of suffering is their main objection to religion. They argue that if God really existed, suffering would not exist. You may think this yourself. Over the next four pages you are going to explore how Muslims reconcile their belief in Allah with the existence of suffering in the world.

You are going to look at four big ideas. These are shown in the Focus Task box.

FOCUS TASK

Make your own large copy of this diagram and make notes on it as you work through the next four pages.

1 Allah has a plan	2 Humans have free will
3 Suffering is a test for the next life	4 Good can come from suffering

✓ CHECKPOINT

Evil
Allah's creation was perfect, so where did evil come from?

According to the Qur'an, Allah also created some unseen beings: JINN, who have free will, and angels, who do not. Allah ordered them to bow down to Adam, since Adam was greater than them. One of the jinn, called Iblis, refused. He was renamed SHAYTAN, which means 'rebellious one'. He tempted Adam and Hawa (Eve) to disobey Allah. To this day Allah allows Shaytan and the jinn who follow him to tempt people away from the path of Allah.

Temptation
Shaytan tempts people into committing evil acts by deceiving them – portraying evil as an attractive thing. However, Muslims must resist Shaytan and evil. Shaytan has no power to *make* people do wrong; only people can choose what to do because they have free will.

Sin
Muslims do not believe in original sin (that people are born with a tendency to evil). Allah gave Adam free will to decide whether to obey Allah. He was tempted by Shaytan and disobeyed Allah, but this did not bring evil into the world. Every baby is born in submission to Allah, so each person has a fresh start. They must choose between right (the guidance of Allah) and wrong (following the temptations of Shaytan).

Forgiveness
Any Muslim who gives in to the temptation of evil can be forgiven if they sincerely repent to Allah.

| 1 Allah has a plan |
| 2 Humans have free will |
| 3 Suffering is a test for the next life |
| 4 Good can come from suffering |

Big idea 1: Allah has a plan

Muslims believe that everything that happens, including suffering, is part of Allah's plan. This belief is called QADR (predestination).

Feature of Qadr			
Allah **knows** everything, that has happened and that will happen in the future	Everything that has happened and is going to happen is **recorded**	Everything happens because **Allah wills** it to happen. Nothing can happen unless Allah wills it	Allah **created** people and created their actions
Example in the Qur'an			
No one knows what he will earn tomorrow; Nor does anyone know in what land he will die. But Allah has full knowledge.	*Do you not know that Allah knows all that is in heaven and on Earth? Indeed it is all in a record, and that is easy for Allah.*	*You shall not will except as Allah wills— The Cherisher of the Worlds.*	*Allah has created you and all your handiwork!*
Surah 31.34	Surah 22.70	Surah 81.29	Surah 37.96

1 Write your own definition of Qadr.
2 Explain the point of the story in Source B.
3 What can Muslims learn about suffering from the example of Muhammad ﷺ?
4 Explain whether you expect to have an easy life or a hard life.
5 Do you think your own life is planned? Explain why some people might have a different point of view.

If everything comes from Allah and nothing happens without Allah's knowledge then those things which humans experience as suffering – death, pain, sorrow – must all be part of a bigger plan that the human mind cannot understand. Whether it is caused by human actions or natural disasters it is still part of Allah's plan.

The example of Muhammad ﷺ

Muhammad ﷺ suffered in his own life. His father died before Muhammad ﷺ was even born, his mother when he was about six. His three sons died very young. His wife Khadijah died when he was only about fifty. He suffered ridicule and death threats from people who did not believe the message of the Qur'an.

Muhammad ﷺ did not blame Allah for his suffering. He was firm in his belief that Allah is responsible for each part of human life – the good and the bad. His example is a model for all Muslims to follow. If Muhammad ﷺ accepted these things as the will of Allah, so should they.

B

Hodja was determined to be decisive and efficient. One day he told his wife he would plough his largest field on the far side of the river and be back for dinner. She urged him to say, 'If Allah is willing.' He told her whether Allah was willing or not, that was his plan. The frightened wife looked up to Allah and asked forgiveness.

Hodja loaded his wooden plough, hitched up the oxen to the wagon, climbed on his donkey, and set off. But within the short span of a day the river flooded from a cloudburst and washed his donkey downstream, and one of the oxen broke a leg in the mud, leaving Hodja to hitch himself in its place to plough the field. Having finished only half the field, at sunset he set out for home exhausted and soaking wet. The river was still high so he had to wait until long past dark to cross over.

After midnight a very wet but much wiser Hodja knocked at his door. 'Who is there?' asked his wife. 'I think it is me, Hodja,' he replied, 'if Allah is willing.'

Many Muslims say 'Inshallah' ('If Allah is willing') when they make plans.

2 Humans have free will

1 Allah has a plan

3 Suffering is a test for the next life	4 Good can come from suffering

Big idea 2: Humans have free will

Every person, Muslim or non-Muslim, has free will to choose whether or not to obey Allah.

You might think that the idea of free will conflicts with the idea of predestination. However, Muslims believe that when they make moral decisions, they make them freely, even though Allah **knows** what the final outcome will be.

Free will is good news and bad news.

Good news – people are not robots

Allah wants people to follow the straight path, but to do so willingly because they love and want to obey Allah, not because they are forced. Without free will, people would simply be like robots or puppets on a string. If Allah stopped people from doing wrong, it would not be a real test of their desire to do right. Nor would they ever learn the importance of the straight way. People learn from their mistakes. A parent can tell a child a thousand times about the dangers of touching a radiator, or pull them away to protect them. But when children are given the freedom to make a mistake and hurt themselves they learn more quickly, if more painfully.

Bad news – free will leads to suffering

The downside of free will is that although some people will follow the path of Allah, some will not – with all its consequences. Muslims believe that departing from the straight path will lead to dreadful consequences – for yourself and for others. If humans cause suffering by disobeying Allah's laws they will be held responsible at the Day of Judgement (which leads us on to Big idea 3).

DISCUSS

1 How is it possible to believe in both free will and Qadr?

2 Is it possible to have free will without suffering?

C

Mischief has appeared on land and sea,
That is what mankind has earned
So that Allah may give them a taste of some of their deeds
in order that they may turn their backs from Evil.

Surah 30.41

ACTIVITY

1 Read **Source C**. It suggests that if people see bad resulting from a wrong decision, they might turn from evil and do good. Draw up a table like the one below.

Wrongdoing – 'Mischief on land and sea'	Consequences – 'taste some of their deeds'	Remedies – 'turn their backs from Evil'

2 Complete the table to show how this process might work in the two situations shown in the cartoons. You could do it like this:

a) discuss with a partner what is happening in each picture

b) for each action, explain why it is wrongdoing (against Allah's will). These ideas go in column 1.

c) explain what consequences might follow in each case. This goes in column 2.

d) explain in column 3 what remedy there might be if the people turned their backs on evil.

3 Add more rows to your table to show how this might work for other examples of human-made suffering.

SAVE AS ...

4 Write a paragraph to explain how far you feel that this process happens in the real world. Show that you have thought about other points of view.

1 Allah has a plan	2 Humans have free will

**3
Suffering is a test for the next life**

	4 Good can come from suffering

Big idea 3: Suffering is a test for the next life

Source D appeared as part of an internet debate about suffering.

D

*The first and perhaps the most important thing to remember is that **this life is not the only life**. There is a better and more lasting life to come. If one has the thought, 'why does Allah make me suffer?' then you must be aware that your suffering in this life is taken into account on Judgement Day and will lighten the punishment or increase the rewards accordingly.*

Suffering is a test for you, as are temptations and many other things in life. If you handle it well and set a good example by showing self control, patience and perseverance, then it is a good deed for which there are rewards. If on the other hand you don't, then you lose out on the rewards.

In general, we should not spend our lives looking at those who are better off but rather at those who are worse off. When we consider those who are worse off than ourselves it helps us to be grateful to Allah for what we have. This continual attitude of gratitude is particularly characteristic of a good Muslim.

1 **Look at the two photos in Source E.**
a) Discuss how and *why* (a) gives a different message from (b), the close-up.
b) Use these pictures as a symbol to explain the way Muslim beliefs in life after death might affect the way Muslims respond to suffering.

Muslims believe that at the Day of Judgement all people will be called to account for their deeds in this life. They will be punished or rewarded accordingly. The judgement will be made by the perfect judge, Allah. So:

- anyone who submits to the will of Allah will not suffer in the long term, even if they do experience suffering in the short term. They will in the end receive perfect justice from Allah.
- anyone who chooses to disobey the will of Allah will suffer in the long term – in their life after death – even if they are happy in the short term – here on Earth.
- no one has a right to happiness or a right to avoid suffering in this life or the next, but people can earn happiness in the next life through what they do in this life.
- individual Muslims should do their best to minimise suffering through their own actions and oppose any actions by others which might cause suffering. Those who have caused evil or suffering by their own actions will be punished. Those who have prevented it will be rewarded.
- in the context of eternity, suffering in this life will not seem so terrible. Indeed in the context of eternity what seems bad now may in fact be for good.

E

(a)

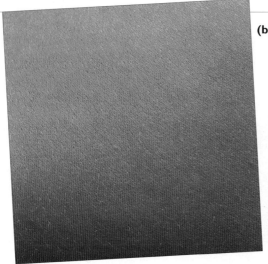

(b)

Skin: (a) as we see it and (b) magnified

<u>B</u>ig idea 4: Good can come from suffering

1 Allah has a plan	2 Humans have free will
3 Suffering is a test for the next life	4 Good can come from suffering

The idea that painful experiences in life are an opportunity is central to the Muslim response to suffering. This might be easy when the link between the suffering and the good outcome is obvious; the pains of childbirth are soon forgotten when the outcome is a healthy new baby. It can be much harder when there is no apparent benefit. It can be particularly hard to explain natural suffering. What good can come out of earthquakes, hurricanes or floods, for example? Or, for that matter, what good can come out of a painful death from cancer?

In Source F Sarah Joseph, a British Muslim, describes her feelings as her mother-in-law was dying from cancer.

F

2 **Read Source F. Write a sentence to describe the attitude to suffering of:**
   a) Sarah's mother-in-law
   b) Sarah
   c) Sarah's husband.
3 **What similarities and differences are there in their reactions to the situation?**
4 **How does her belief in**
   a) life after death
   b) a Day of Judgement appear to affect Sarah Joseph's response to this situation?
   You can find out more about these beliefs on page 52.
5 **What good opportunities arise from this situation according to Sarah Joseph?**

FOCUS TASK

Over the last four pages you have made notes on your copy of the diagram from page 41. You are now going to use those notes to make a four-panel wall display. Work in four groups. Each group take one big idea. Write the big idea in really big letters in the centre of your panel. Write the supporting evidence or ideas around it. Include pictures, quotations and your own explanations.

My mother-in-law's cancer – an ever-present monster – takes more of her every day. I curse it as if it has an identity. What right does it have to hurt her? [5]

My thoughts and my emotions are very confused. I have never seen anyone die before. Stupid! We are all dying. But that death is so far away. This death though is tangible. I am [10] always ready for it, poised to cope …

I watch her children care for her, and I am grateful to Allah. I pray mine care for me when I am old and frail.

I often sit and watch her laboured [15] breath and think, 'Is this the last one?' It will probably take me unawares when it does happen – and only Allah knows when that will be. Two years ago, the doctors said, 'Six months!' But they [20] were not aware of her sheer will to survive.

'Death will find us all' – the Qur'an tells us that, but as we fritter away our precious time we fail to see the grains [25] of sand in the hour-glass pass away. Occasionally someone we love dies – we are reminded of our own mortality. But we forget as quickly as we remembered. Death – the only [30] absolute in our lives. Yet we think so little of it, scared to think.

But more than death there is the dying. The same thing? Most definitely not. I feel a shiver. To pass away [35] quietly in one's sleep after having lived a long and fulfilling life – don't we all wish for something like that? But there may be some other fate waiting for us and how would we bear it? Where [40] there is pain and suffering, my mother-in-law bears it with strength and dignity. She has always had patience and I remind myself, 'train yourself in patience whilst life is easy, for later, [45] when life is hard, you will need it.'

One could ask why? I have been left without answers. I have scolded Allah and He has remained silent. Or has He? No – He has talked to me as He [50] has talked to everybody. He has spoken through the Qur'an, if we but bother to look and listen. He has told us: 'What is the life of this world but amusement and play? Truly the home [55] in the hereafter, that is life indeed, if they only knew.' (29.64) But we fail to listen and we do not use the opportunities – however small they may seem. [60]

My husband describes the situation as an opportunity for us to earn reward as we look after her. An opportunity for us to strengthen our character. And, not least, an opportunity for her to free [65] herself of sin. Have I made the most of this opportunity? I do not know, but I am trying – trying to give back some of the love which she has given me. She has always treated me with kindness, [70] not caring that I am English, not caring that I cannot speak her mother tongue. Only caring that I was Muslim and I tried to communicate in ways beyond words … She has given out love and [75] thus she receives it – in this life, and I pray with confidence that she will receive it in the Hereafter.

Sarah Joseph was formerly editor of *Trends* (see page 7). This is from her editorial for Volume 7, Issue 2.

Thinking about Allah – Review tasks

A

How might Muslims answer those who say there is no God?

There are many reasons why people do not believe in God. These are some of the things that people say:

> I cannot believe in a God whom I have not heard or seen. If God exists, surely I would have heard from him by now . . .

> I cannot believe in God. There is too much suffering in this world . . .

> I cannot believe in God. Science and modern ideas have disproved religion . . .

> I cannot believe in God. The people who follow God are not a good advertisement for him . . .

In Units 1 and 2, you found out about some of the basic beliefs of Islam. Write a reply to one of the speakers, expressing Muslim beliefs about these issues.

B

Ibadah

1 Explain what the people in the picture are doing.
2 Explain why it is an act of ibadah.
3 Describe two other activities, done regularly by Muslims, that would also be called ibadah.
4 Choose one act of ibadah and write a paragraph to explain how it might help Muslims to develop their consciousness of Allah?
5 Do you agree that everything a person does can be an act of worship? Give reasons to support your view and explain why other people may disagree.

At this mosque in Marseilles (France), there are sometimes so many worshippers that the Friday prayers spill out into the street.

UNIT 3

Issues of life and death

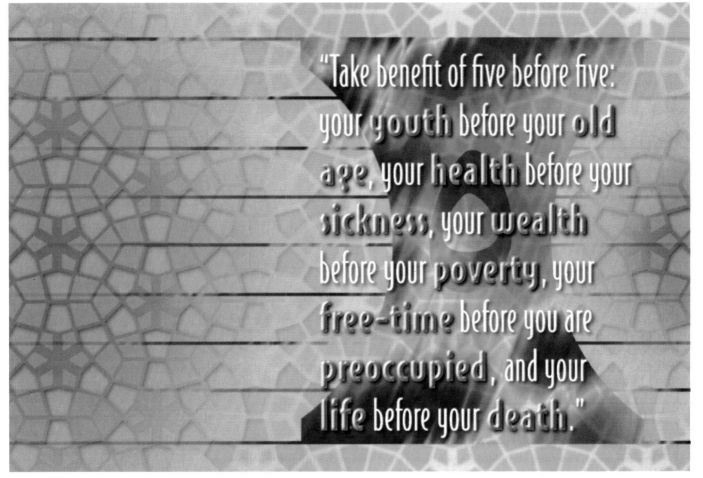

"Take benefit of five before five: your youth before your old age, your health before your sickness, your wealth before your poverty, your free-time before you are preoccupied, and your life before your death."

A saying of Muhammad 鑿. It comes from a series of postcards published in Britain, called 'Pearls of the Prophet', which give extracts from the Hadith

Muslims believe that Allah is the source of all life. But in today's society human beings seem to have greater power over life and death than ever before. There seem to be more opportunities for ordinary people to make choices about life and death. For example, 40 years ago abortion was illegal in Britain. Now it is legal. A decision which used to be taken for you is now left to the individual. Muslims would say that making something legal does not make it morally acceptable.

In this unit you are going to see how their faith guides Muslims in making decisions about life and death. You are also going to make up your own mind about how far Muslim ideas can help non-Muslims make moral decisions. Don't discard what you have already studied. As you work through this unit you will find yourself referring back many times to the ideas you studied in Units 1 and 2. These are the foundation stones for understanding Muslim responses to moral issues.

How do Muslim beliefs about death affect the living?

Moona Taslim-Saif works for Taslim Funerals which is based in the grounds of the East London Mosque in Whitechapel, London. The company was founded by her grandfather.

B   How I got started …

When I was younger, my great-uncle asked me to go to the mortuary to switch off the lights. I remember opening the door, and there were stillborn twin babies lying there. I screamed.

They were always freaking me out. I'd jump in the van and then realise that behind me was a dead body! I really didn't like it at all.

One day a mother came in to the office who had lost a seven-year-old daughter through cancer. She was in a real state and came in to wash the girl's body. She was crying on me and I had to take her to the mortuary. I thought, 'I can't just chuck her in there and leave her.' So I took a deep breath and went in.

I had to completely bluff my way through, as if I'd always been dealing with dead bodies. I ended up doing the wash with her.

I knew what to do because my grandma had often told me. It is quite simple, because it is the same as the special wash a woman performs after her period or after she has had sex. So that is how I got started.

I went to Leeds to train to be a teacher. I taught in a school in Pudsey and then I came back to London and worked with kids with special needs, because that's what I enjoy doing. I was short of work for a couple of weeks and Dad said, 'Just come in and give me a hand.' He really wanted a member of his family to work with him. I said, 'Fine, but I will not have anything to do with the dead bodies.'

When I saw the state of the office, I thought, 'Oh my God, what a nightmare! I've got to sort this out.' I thought I'd be here for about three or four months, but that was three and a half years ago . . .

C   Attitudes to death …

A lot of clients appear not to be that affected by death. The men come in and they say, 'I want this and this. There's the money,' and we'll say, 'We'll see you at the cemetery.' They don't want any input and they don't want you to do any extra counselling. They know how it works and they know there's a job to be done and they just do it.

Other clients are not quite sure what is going on. They are looking for answers to questions. That is when you start telling them what Islam says about death, and other ideas to do with the religion. They learn a lot in just the couple of days they are dealing with us.

A lot of times when mothers lose children, they can't focus on anything. You start telling them stories you have read: the idea

that in heaven the Prophet Muhammad ﷺ is sitting under a tree and all the children sit there with him and Allah asks them, What can I do for you now? And the children say, 'Bring my Mum and Dad.' People often say that losing a child is your ticket to heaven; the child will call for you to be with them and you will go to heaven, so in a way it is a blessing in disguise. A lot of people find that very comforting.

Although I was brought up in a funeral-directing family, I don't have the same attitude that my grandad had towards death. He had such faith, he believed that death is part of life – it wasn't really a problem. I think that is amazing and I hope that one day I can feel that way too.

D   When grief takes over ...

So you do get extremes. Some people quickly forget all about it and carry on as they were before. Then you get other people whose lives are changed completely.

I had one particular case. A young Mauritian lady. She lost her husband very suddenly when he was just 27. She was left with two severely disabled children. The boy had nine operations during his life, so when he went into hospital again no one thought it was serious. She hardly left his bedside, but she went to the toilet and when she came back he had passed away. She was devastated. She went a bit strange after that. Her life revolved around those two children, her whole day had been just caring for them. She actually went a bit mad with it. When the boy died she spent every night in the mortuary here. Then the coffin went home because she wanted to spend one more evening with him before the funeral. Her friend phoned me and said, 'She is in the coffin with her son.'

I had to go round to the house and there she was, a room full of people and she was in the coffin with her son. Everyone was thinking, What the hell do we do here? No one would approach her. If it had been one of my family, I probably wouldn't have known what to do, but because it was someone I don't know that well, I could be a little more detached.

I went straight over to her. I didn't tell her to get out of the coffin. I talked to her while she was in there. It was at that point that I started to talk to her about Islam, she didn't know much about it. I said, 'He is a child, he is going straight to heaven. He was under so much strain here. He is in a much better place. You should feel happy for him.'

There is this whole thing in Islam that you shouldn't cry over a dead body and she was wailing and everything. We sat there and we chatted. I phoned up the cemetery and told them we were going to be delayed. I told everyone to just chill out. 'We are not going to rush it. She is burying her son and she just can't cope with it.'

I had to do a hell of a lot of religious counselling with her, I even phoned up my mother to check that what I was saying was right. In the end it was all sorted, the funeral went off smoothly. Afterwards she started to phone me regularly and ask me loads of questions about Islam. I told her, 'You really need to get yourself attached to a mosque where there is an imam who can give you guidance, regular guidance.' She has now become very religious.

ACTIVITY

1   **Read Sources B–E. How has Moona's attitude changed towards death?**
2   **What do you think has caused this change?**
3   **Muslims carefully wash a person after death and dress them in a shroud of white cloth. The body may be visited before the funeral.**
    In groups, discuss how this might help the bereaved to cope with the death of their loved ones.

SAVE AS ...

4   **Draft a leaflet advertising Taslim Funerals to bereaved Muslims. Be sure to mention what is specifically Muslim about the service they offer. Think about the needs of different clients and try to be sensitive to these needs.**

E   Washing the body ...

You get a lot of strength from washing the bodies. I have to be in the mood to do it, but I love doing it. Before you go in there, you think you are going to be really scared, but actually it is quite therapeutic because at that point you feel really close to God. You are giving them their last bath, it is all very gentle and it is done with so much care. I tend to do it when the family come in, I do it with them. A lot of times they need to be talked through it. It is a very special moment for them.

I have only had one person who couldn't do it, you would think it would be exactly the opposite. A lot of them say, 'I don't know if I can do it,' so I say, 'Tell you what, turn up. If you come and you can't do it, you can always walk out, but if you don't go in there, you might always think, I wish I'd tried.'

They come in and give a goodbye kiss and I say, 'Here's the shampoo, why don't you wash Mum's hair?' and before you know it, the tears have dried up and they are saying, 'She has got lovely hair, hasn't she?'. I'll say, 'It's in lovely condition,' or 'It hasn't gone at all grey,' or whatever. And then I'll suggest, 'Why don't you say these prayers, read the Shahadah to her. It's to coach her, because when she goes to the grave she'll be asked questions.'

1 Read the Checkpoint below. How do you think *you* would be judged?

✓ CHECKPOINT

The Day of Judgement

Muslims believe that this life is a preparation for the eternal life to come (AKHIRAH). On a particular day, which Allah has chosen, life on Earth will come to an end; everything will be destroyed. On that day, all the people who have ever lived will be raised from the dead and judged by Allah.

If the good deeds a person has done in their life outweigh the bad things, that person will go to paradise (heaven); if not, the person will be punished in hell for their bad deeds. In making the judgement even a person's intentions (niyyah) are taken into account:

- if a person has the intention to do a good deed but is unable to carry it out, Allah records it as a good deed
- but if he has intended it and done it, Allah records it as ten good deeds
- but if a person has intended a bad deed and has not done it, Allah records it as a good deed
- but if he has intended it and has done it, Allah records it as one bad deed.

Hadith Qudsi

Muslims believe that Allah is merciful and forgiving, so even the people who have been bad will be allowed into paradise when they have been punished and are truly sorry for what they have done. However, some Muslims say that there are some things people do that are so bad they may not be forgiven, such as 'SHIRK', the sin of believing in something other than Allah at the time of death.

FOCUS TASK

Your beliefs usually have an impact on your attitudes and values. These in turn affect what you do – your actions. Your actions have an impact on other people. Is this true of belief in life after death and the Day of Judgement?

Copy and complete the following chart to show the way that these beliefs might affect the believers' actions, and how these actions might affect other people.

The possible effect of believing in life after death and the Day of Judgement on your attitudes to ...	On your actions ...	Impact of these actions on other people
Bereavement It helps you to cope with death because you know there is the life to come	At my grandfather's funeral, I . . .	
Honesty It stops you being dishonest because you know Allah sees everything you do and will judge you for it	When I found a purse on a train . . .	
Possessions It makes you realise that material possessions are temporary and not the source of true happiness	When I look for a job. . .	
Suffering It gives you the determination to rise above problems in this life because you know life is a test	When my life is hard, I . . .	
Personal responsibility It forces you to think about people other than yourself and your responsibilities towards the whole of creation	When deciding what to do with my leisure time, I . . .	

Good

Bad

You are now going to look at how Muslims apply these beliefs to the issues of abortion (pages 53–5), euthanasia (pages 56–9) and capital punishment (pages 60–63).

3.2 Can abortion ever be justified?

Sumayah's choice

This is a true story which happened in Britain in the 1990s.

Sumayah was in her late twenties when she found she was pregnant with her third child. She was still less than three months pregnant when she caught chicken-pox. She was not particularly ill with the virus, but she suffered a high temperature for a few days and had the inevitable blisters. Sumayah was concerned that it might have caused damage to the developing fetus. She discussed the problem with her husband on the telephone. He was overseas at the time, on a lecture tour. He offered to come home, but Sumayah said that as several members of their family lived near by, they could help her if she needed support.

Sumayah carefully studied the leaflets and books which the hospital had given her, but found no reference to chicken-pox at all. She reread the notes about rubella (german measles) and was disturbed by the harrowing descriptions of the damage rubella can cause to unborn children: stillbirth (the baby being born dead), miscarriage, deafness, blindness and a range of other abnormalities.

With this in mind, she decided to go to the hospital's antenatal clinic for advice. At the clinic, the news sounded positive. 'No,' she was told, 'chicken-pox is unlikely to cause a problem.' She wanted to feel reassured, but the nagging doubts in her mind wouldn't go away. That evening after she had said du'a for her children and put them to bed, she sat down to think.

Suddenly a thought came into her mind: her uncle! The one who spent so much time studying Islam. The one who had always been so patient with her questions about Islam. That uncle was not only very knowledgeable about the Qur'an, but was also in his working life an obstetrician! She dialled his number.

The conversation that followed was not a happy one. It confirmed Sumayah's worst fears. Certainly chicken-pox could cause problems if you were pregnant, especially if it caused a very high temperature. Her uncle carefully explained the different Islamic views on the subject, advised her to have an ultrasound scan immediately and to be prepared to make a decision about an abortion. Sadly, the scan revealed that Sumayah's baby was seriously deformed.

ACTIVITY

1 Read the flowchart on pages 54–5. In pairs or small groups discuss each issue Sumayah needs to consider and the questions which follow it.
2 What do you think Sumayah *should* do?
3 What do you think Sumayah *will* do?

SAVE AS ...

4 **Either:**
Write a conversation between Sumayah and her uncle after Sumayah has decided what to do. Sumayah should explain her decision with reference to Islamic teaching. (She should show that she is aware of different opinions within Islam).
Or:
Write up your opinion as advice to Sumayah, carefully justifying it with reference to Islamic teaching.

PS Your teacher can tell you what Sumayah decided to do.

A

O mankind! We created you out of dust, then out of sperm, then out of a leech-like clot, then out of a morsel of flesh, partly formed and partly unformed, in order to show Our power to you;
We cause whom we will to stay in the wombs for a certain term, then We bring you out as babies …

Surah 22.5

As a Muslim, Sumayah believes that life is sacred and is in Allah's hands. Allah creates all life. Only Allah can decide when life should end. She knows that Muhammad 醫 says in the Hadith, 'Whoever severs the womb-relationship ties, I will sever my ties with him' (Bukhari Hadith 78.13) and the Qur'an says 'Do not take life – which Allah has made sacred – except for a just cause.' (17.33). But is this a just cause?

The Qur'an is quite specific that abortion for purely economic reasons is not permitted: 'Do not kill your children for fear of want' (17.31). Muslims would argue that Allah will always provide for what He has created. But all Muslims permit abortion if the aim is to save the life of the mother and some have said that it is also permissible if there is a strong likelihood of a serious deformity or disease in the child. However, others say that aborting a fetus because it might be disabled is wrong and that Allah understands things we cannot. There is a purpose in that child's life, however difficult it is for us to understand.

Issue 1
Does Islam allow abortion?

What do you think? Would Islam allow this abortion? Would it be for 'a just cause' (a good reason)?

Issue 2
When does life begin?

B

We believe that the soul is breathed in by the first 42 days of pregnancy. What has led us to this opinion is the hard fact of embryology, that all stages – seed, clot of blood and morsel of flesh [see Source A] occur in the first 40 days of life; so, the interpretation of some Muslim scholars has to be wrong.

A. Majid Katme, Muslim Coordinator of The Society for the Protection of the Unborn Child, in *Q-News*, 28 May 1993

Life doesn't begin at one specific moment. The potential for human life grows with the fetus.

- Life begins before conception (when Allah plans that a life should begin).

- Life begins at conception (when fertilized egg implants in the womb lining).

- Life begins after 25 days when the heart of the fetus starts to beat.

- Life begins after 12 weeks when all of the organs of the body are formed.

- Life begins after 120 days when, according to Hadith, life is breathed into the fetus.

- Life begins at 23 weeks when the fetus can survive outside its mother with medical help.

- Life begins when the baby is born. This usually happens naturally about 9 months after conception.

Look at the chart. When would you say life begins? Sumayah's fetus is less than 90 days old. What advice do you think Sumayah would receive from the writers of Sources B and C?

Fetus in womb by Sharajudiv Sabuncuoglu (1790)

C

According to An-Nawawi's Hadith 4: Before 120 days from conception, the fetus lacks a human soul. Only at the end of 120 days is the fetus ensouled. To consider in the same light abortions that are performed before the 120-day period and after as the [Anti-Abortion lobby does] is therefore both ridiculous and unIslamic. Muslim jurists prohibit, absolutely, any abortion taking place after ensoulment (when the soul enters the body), but many of them permit it before 120 days under certain conditions (the poor health of the mother, in the case of rape, etc.).

N. Mahjoub in *Q-News*, 14 May 1993

Issue 4
What effect will my decision have on the quality of life of others?

Sumayah's decision will affect the lives of the following: her husband, her other children, her family.

What do you think?
Would anyone's quality of life be greatly harmed if Sumayah had an abortion? Whose 'quality of life' *should* be most considered here?

Issue 3
What can I learn from this suffering?

Islam teaches that people should not *expect* life to be enjoyable; there is a point to Sumayah's suffering. The same goes for the deformed fetus in her womb – there is a purpose to its suffering too. Sumayah must view this as a test. The life after death is in every way more important than this life, so Sumayah must follow Allah's guidance in this situation.

What do you think?
What can Sumayah learn from this? Would Sumayah be ducking out of the test if she had an abortion?

Issue 5
Do I have a right to choose?

Some say that a woman has a right to say what happens to her body and that right takes priority over the rights of the fetus. She alone should have the freedom to choose whether or not she wants to terminate the pregnancy. Most Muslims would not support this view.

What do you think?
Who else might have rights to influence Sumayah's decision?

Issue 6
What is my intention?

DISCUSS

Look at these situations. What might be the woman's intentions if she sought an abortion in each case? Discuss why these intentions might or might not be acceptable to Allah.

1) **A woman has six children already, two have died of malnutrition.**
2) **The father has just died.**
3) **The woman was raped.**
4) **The woman is 14 years old.**
5) **The woman is in the middle of a degree course and wants to complete it.**
6) **The woman will probably die if she continues with the pregnancy.**
7) **The woman does not want any children at all.**
8) **The woman has a physically disabled son already and has been told that if she has another boy there is a one in two risk that he will be physically disabled too.**

Muslims believe that on the Day of Judgement, Allah will take into consideration someone's niyyah (intention) when judging their actions. So if Sumayah has an abortion for reasons Allah judges to be good, those reasons would count in her favour.

What do you think?
What are Sumayah's intentions?

3.3 Why is euthanasia forbidden in Islam?

Look at Source A. This soldier has paid a high price in his country's civil war. His pain makes him scream uncontrollably at night. He tells anybody who will listen that he wishes he was dead. His doctors give him little chance of survival. His family have disappeared. His home has been destroyed.

Some people would argue that this man should have the right to die – to put an end to his misery. Why should he be kept alive when he has clearly stated his wish to die?

A

A critically wounded Muslim

✓ CHECKPOINT

What is euthanasia?
Euthanasia is the term used to describe ending a person's life deliberately, but for compassionate reasons.

Euthanasia in Britain
Euthanasia is illegal in Britain. There have been a number of attempts to get a bill through Parliament legalising euthanasia. All have failed. One example was a bill in 1969. If it had been passed, it would have allowed euthanasia on request to anyone over 18, provided that 'two doctors believed the patient to be suffering from a serious physical illness or impairment, reasonably thought to be incurable, and expected to cause considerable distress'.

VOLUNTARY EUTHANASIA is when a person asks for their own life to be ended.

COMPULSORY or INVOLUNTARY EUTHANASIA is when someone else, e.g. a doctor or a family member, decides that it would be in the person's best interest to end their life.

ACTIVE EUTHANASIA is when something is done to the person to make them die more quickly, e.g. giving drugs to bring about death.

PASSIVE EUTHANASIA is when any form of treatment which might extend a person's life is taken away, e.g. turning off a life support machine or removing a feeding tube. N.B. In Britain today this is allowed. It would not legally be termed euthanasia.

ACTIVITY
Imagine you are a doctor and this man is your patient. You are moved by his terrible physical condition. You hear him say, 'I wish I was dead.' Would you help him to die or would you do all you could to keep him alive?

Write a paragraph as if you are talking to the man. You should explain what you have decided and the reasons for your decision.

FOCUS TASK

1   Use the definitions in the Checkpoint to describe correctly the different 'fates' below:

Fate 1
The doctor agrees to the soldier's request. He injects the soldier with a lethal drug and the soldier dies within hours.

Fate 2
The soldier has become unconscious. The doctor decides to end the soldier's life. He injects a lethal drug and the soldier dies within hours.

Fate 3
The soldier is unconscious and the doctor decides to help the soldier die. He removes the drip and stops the medicines which are keeping the soldier alive. The soldier dies two days later.

Fate 4
The doctor helps the soldier to accept his suffering. He supports him medically with painkillers and spiritually with prayer until his death.

2   Which fates do you think are morally acceptable? Compare your ideas with others in the class.
3   Which fates are legal in Britain? You will need to refer to the Checkpoint.
4   Supporters of euthanasia often call it 'mercy killing'. Opponents describe it as 'legal murder'. Which description do you think is more accurate? Explain why.
5   What case could be made for saying that euthanasia is always wrong?

What religious questions are raised for Muslims by this issue?

Euthanasia is an issue which raises many basic religious questions.

* Why do people suffer?
* Why does Allah allow suffering to continue?
* Does my life belong to me or to Allah?

What does Islam teach?

Islam makes an absolute moral judgement regarding euthanasia, arguing that it is always wrong. So the issue for Muslims is not what to decide, but to understand *why* it is forbidden. As always, Muslims will base their understanding on the teachings of the Qur'an and the Hadith. These are the main points of their argument:

1 Allah has a plan

Everything in the universe has been created by Allah for a purpose (see page 42). In the same way, every human being was born for a reason, with a part to play. This reason is known only to Allah.

2 Euthanasia would disrupt Allah's plan

As part of his plan for the universe, Allah has already decided how long everyone is to live. It is not for the individual to decide. Allah's plan might involve suffering. This does not mean that Allah is cruel. Muslims believe Allah is compassionate. Allah alone knows the reasons for the suffering and tests we go through. Good things can come out of suffering.

B

O you who believe! Seek help with patient perseverance and prayer, for Allah is with those who patiently persevere … We shall test you with fear and hunger, loss of goods or lives or the fruits of your labour; but give glad tidings to those who patiently persevere, who say, when afflicted with calamity, 'To Allah we belong and … return.'

Surah 2.153–6

The natural world is ordered and arranged according to Allah's will. The patterns you can see in the natural world are a sign of Allah's plan.

3 Allah knows best

Any person asking to die or making the decision for someone to die is claiming to know better than Allah that the person is ready for death. But they do not: Allah alone knows. It is therefore not merciful to kill a person before their appointed time; you could be destroying Allah's plan. This is true even if a person is in great pain. All Muslims should obey Allah's will and should trust in Allah's mercy.

4 Voluntary euthanasia is a form of suicide

Many Muslims would regard voluntary euthanasia as suicide. Suicide is condemned in Islam. Muhammad ﷺ expressed this belief very clearly (Source C).

Many Muslims believe that on the Day of Judgement voluntary euthanasia will cause a person's soul to be treated in the same way as if they had committed suicide.

C

Whoever commits suicide with something will be punished with the same thing in the (hell) fire

Bukhari Hadith 78.647

D

How do Muslims care for the terminally ill?

Compassion for the suffering is very important to Muslims. So the second issue facing a Muslim caring for a terminally ill person is to deal with practical problems which might arise for the suffering patient or their family.

Terminally ill Muslims in Britain are more likely to be cared for by families at home than in hospices. This is because the family is very important in Islam and children grow up in the knowledge that members of a family are there to support each other (see pages 70–71). It is a religious duty to provide for parents in times of need and to help make their lives as comfortable as possible. Muslims might feel they were neglecting their relatives if they did not give them the care they needed at home. In recent years however, some hospices have reported an increasing number of Muslim patients. The team that provides spiritual support for patients at the North London Hospice includes Christians, Jews and Muslims.

E

DYING WOMAN PLEADS FOR DIGNITY AT THE LAST

Annie Lindsell is living on borrowed time. She suffers from the terminal illness motor neurone disease and is enduring a long deterioration into death.

Week by week, her life changes for the worse. She can no longer go to the bathroom alone, or dress herself or wash. She notices she can no longer grip a cup as she once did. She fears eating out will soon become too embarrassing to contemplate: 'I end up wearing more food than eating it,' she says. It is the lack of dignity she hates most.

She is brave and determined but knows that, barring a miracle cure, her prognosis is not good. Most sufferers survive just three years from diagnosis. She has already lasted four. But when the time comes, she wants to die quickly.

Next week she will appear at the House of Commons to explain why she believes there should be a change in the law so that she can die at a time and in a manner she chooses.

Annie, 45, plans to explain what it is like to know that you are going to die young, in a painful or humiliating way, and that your preferred death – with dignity – is forbidden by law. 'I've had a wonderful life over which I've had control,' she says, 'Now I want a dignified death over which I have control, too.

'I've lost 15 friends with AIDS and both my parents with cancer. These people can end up in a state of drugged oblivion and they still take days if not weeks to die. This is not something I expect in a civilised society. Is it really where the best interests of the patients lie?'

Annie does not want to die and certainly not yet. 'I'm not just sitting in a depressed state thinking about nothing but death. But I can see my deterioration. Every week there is something.

One week I can pick up a cup, next week it's difficult and the following week I can't do it at all.'

As the law stands, she faces a huge dilemma. 'Do I do something about this while I still can or do I wait until the thing progresses and discover that I'm right and that I cannot bear the quality of my life?'

Nearly half of the doctors questioned in one survey said they would help a terminally ill person die if it were legal. She and fellow campaigners believe it would be feasible to draw up strict rules to govern cases of people suffering incurable illnesses who would like medical help to end their suffering.

The option should apply only to the terminally ill, she says. They would have had to express their desire to die over a period of time, not just once in depression. Two doctors should back the decision and the police and judiciary should be informed. In Holland, where such deaths are allowed, there has been no 'slippery slope' extension of the rules, she says.

Ideally, she would like to die with her close family and friends around her. She wants to do so 'with peace and dignity' and argues her quality of life would improve today if she knew it was possible.

An article from the *Independent on Sunday*, 21 January 1996

DISCUSS

Having studied Muslim views on euthanasia, what do you now think about these key questions:

1 **How can a compassionate God allow people to suffer?**
2 **In what ways can good come out of suffering?**
3 **Is it better to have absolute or relative moral values in making decisions about euthanasia?**
4 **Is voluntary euthanasia murder or mercy killing?**

Read Source E. How do you react to Annie Lindsell's plea? Annie's doctor, Dr Simon Holmes, felt that the law was so unclear that he could not give her the treatment they both felt would allow her to die with dignity. Annie decided to seek a legal judgment. The case received much publicity and was discontinued when it became clear that the treatment the doctor proposed was simply following the 'responsible body of good medical practice'.

The result was that Annie was able to live her last remaining weeks safe in the knowledge that, should it become necessary, her doctor would legally be able to give her the distress-relieving drugs that would shorten her life.

Annie Lindsell passed away peacefully in December 1997 from respiratory failure caused by the progression of motor neurone disease.

FOCUS TASK A

Imagine that you are a Muslim in discussion with Annie Lindsell or another person suffering from an incurable disease who wants to choose when to die.

This person is not a Muslim and knows nothing of Muslim beliefs. Write a conversation you might have in which you explain how Allah views the situation. You will need to argue that:

1 **you understand that there is a lot of pain and that you sympathise**
2 **despite the pain, Allah really is the Merciful and the Compassionate**
3 **good can come out of suffering.**

Use the information on pages 57–8 in your explanation. Include as many ideas as you can from Sources B–D.

FOCUS TASK B

'Allah is compassionate. There is always a reason for suffering.'

Write an essay to explain how far you agree or disagree with this statement. Your answer should not only explain your own point of view, but also explain the opposite point of view and why you reject it.

Try to base one paragraph on each column on this diagram.

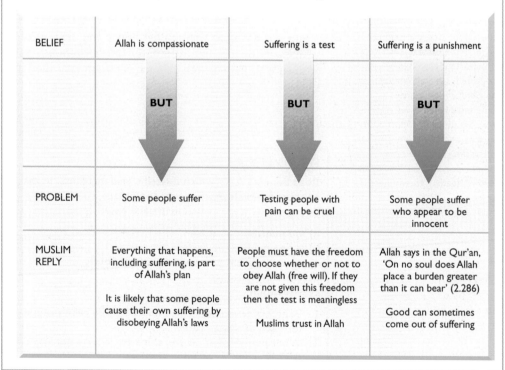

BELIEF	Allah is compassionate	Suffering is a test	Suffering is a punishment
	BUT	**BUT**	**BUT**
PROBLEM	Some people suffer	Testing people with pain can be cruel	Some people suffer who appear to be innocent
MUSLIM REPLY	Everything that happens, including suffering, is part of Allah's plan It is likely that some people cause their own suffering by disobeying Allah's laws	People must have the freedom to choose whether or not to obey Allah (free will). If they are not given this freedom then the test is meaningless Muslims trust in Allah	Allah says in the Qur'an, 'On no soul does Allah place a burden greater than it can bear' (2.286) Good can sometimes come out of suffering

3.4 Is it ever right to kill a human being as a punishment?

A

GHOLAMEZA KHOSHROU WAS A PERSISTENT AND DEVIOUS CRIMINAL

Khoshrou had been arrested many times during his life and charged with theft, kidnapping, forgery and rape. Somehow he had avoided heavy punishments by always using assumed names to conceal his previous criminal record.

In 1993 he escaped justice again. He was arrested and charged with kidnapping and rape, but escaped before his trial.

Later he was not so lucky; he served a prison term, but again using a false identity, and so avoided the full force of the law.

After being released from prison, Khoshrou continued his criminal activities. He stole a car and pretended to be a taxi driver. He collected his victims late at night and early in the morning and began a reign of terror using the vehicle termed his 'death sleigh'.

His campaign of rape and murder continued for a period of four months and resulted in the deaths of nine women.

In court, he was found guilty of theft, kidnapping, rape and nine counts of murder.

B

GITI WAS LOOKING AFTER HER FIVE-YEAR-OLD NEPHEW, SHARWIN

She was trying to vacuum her house and the boy kept misbehaving. Giti tried to get Sharwin to stop, but eventually lost her temper. She hit him over the head several times with the vacuum cleaner. Sharwin later died in hospital from his injuries.

C

ONE NIGHT ALI ASGHAR WAS LEFT ALONE with his two-month-old baby daughter Malika after a big row with his wife. His wife returned home a few days later and was unable to find her husband or daughter, so she contacted the police. Later, Asghar confessed that he had killed Malika and thrown her body out into the street.

ACTIVITY A

Read Sources A–C, which describe real incidents. In the country in which these events took place, the following punishments were available in each case:

a) no punishment at all
b) a fine paid to the state
c) compensation paid to the victim's family
d) a prison sentence
e) execution.

1 Which of these punishments would *you* recommend for each of these crimes?
2 What punishment do you think the courts did impose? Give reasons for all your answers.

Islam and capital punishment

The cases in Sources A–C took place in the Islamic Republic of Iran. The reason that the Iranian courts can sentence people to death is because they apply Shari'ah (Islamic law). The Shari'ah is always based on teaching in the Qur'an and the Hadith. However, many conditions have to be met before a person can be executed and, as you can see from Source D, other punishments are available. The death penalty is rarely carried out and only ever as a punishment for murder (which is premeditated), not for manslaughter (which is not planned).

D

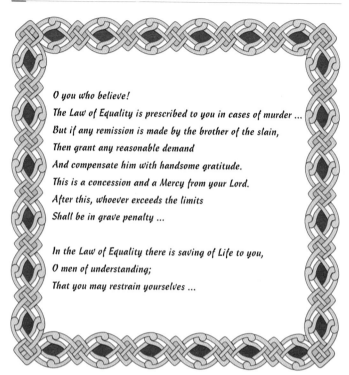

O you who believe!

The Law of Equality is prescribed to you in cases of murder ...

But if any remission is made by the brother of the slain,

Then grant any reasonable demand

And compensate him with handsome gratitude.

This is a concession and a Mercy from your Lord.

After this, whoever exceeds the limits

Shall be in grave penalty ...

In the Law of Equality there is saving of Life to you,

O men of understanding;

That you may restrain yourselves ...

Surah 2.178–9

ACTIVITY B

1   On a copy of **Source D**, label the phrases that support the following principles.
    a) **If someone murders they should be killed in return.**
    b) **The family of the victim can spare the murderer and prevent the death sentence being carried out.**
    c) **Capital punishment is an effective deterrent against murder.**
    d) **A murderer who is spared the death penalty must pay compensation instead.**
    e) **Capital punishment helps people to develop self-control.**
    f) **Allah is forgiving and so allows for compensation to be paid.**
2   a) **On your sheet, highlight the three features in Question 1 which are distinctively Islamic. Use the Checkpoint on page 60 to help you.**
    b) **Explain why some people might agree or disagree with each feature.**
3   Revise with a partner the Muslim teaching on life after death (see page 52). Do you think this would encourage or discourage Islamic courts from carrying out executions? Explain your answer.
4   Compare your sentences on the cases in Sources A–C with those of the Iranian courts.
    The judgments:

    •   **Source A – Gholameza Khoshrou was executed on 13 August 1998.**
    •   **Source B – Giti was convicted of the manslaughter of her nephew Sharwin. She was sentenced to three years in prison.**
    •   **Source C – the father, Ali Asghar, paid compensation for the murder of his daughter Malika.**

    Explain why you think your sentences are similar to or different from what happened in real life.

ACTIVITY C

Before attempting this task, make sure you have read the Checkpoint on page 60 and the text at the top of this page.

If someone were found guilty of murdering a member of your family, would you insist on execution?

In 1997, Frank Gilford, an Australian citizen, was faced with this situation: his sister Yvonne, a nurse working in Saudi Arabia, had been brutally murdered. Two British women, Deborah Parry and Lucille McLaughlan, who had worked with Yvonne, were charged with her murder and so Mr Gilford was forced to consider whether to insist on execution or accept compensation instead.

1   Put yourself in Frank Gilford's shoes. What should you do if:
    a) you wish to be merciful
    b) you wish to honour your sister
    c) you wish to prevent another tragedy
    d) you doubt that the accused women are guilty?
    Explain your answers.
2   How might your decision be affected by considering:
    a) your own peace of mind
    b) Lucille McLaughlan and Deborah Parry
    c) the families of these two nurses
    d) your dead sister?
3   In groups, role play a debate on the advantages and disadvantages of the victim's family being involved in decisions about punishment. You should consider what you have learnt about the Islamic view.

ACTIVITY

Work in groups.

1 Write each of the following statements on a separate slip of paper.
2 Draw a scale like the one on the right on a large piece of paper.
3 As a group, try to decide where to place each statement.

```
 -5  -4  -3  -2  -1   0   1   2   3   4   5
 |   |   |   |   |   |   |   |   |   |   |
Strongly              Not              Strongly
disagree             sure                agree
```

a)

> If someone kills, they should be killed in return.

b)

> No legal system is perfect; mistakes are made and people are occasionally wrongly convicted. If capital punishment was allowed then an innocent person would sometimes be killed.

c)

> Capital punishment is a good deterrent. If you know you might be hanged, you'll think twice before killing someone.

d)

> Capital punishment doesn't work as a deterrent; look at the countries where they allow the death penalty – there are still plenty of murders.

e)

> If we allow capital punishment, that makes us as bad as the killer. Retribution is just another name for revenge, and that should not be allowed in a civilised society.

f)

> I believe that any killing is wrong, including capital punishment.

g)

> Capital punishment gives a clear message that a society totally disapproves of murder.

h)

> What is the point of capital punishment? Killing the killer is not going to bring the victim back to life.

i)

> I am opposed to capital punishment. Any punishment for a crime should aim to reform that person. We should never say that a person is beyond help.

j)

> People have to be protected from killers. The only way to be sure that a killer won't kill again is to end their life.

k)

> I am not sure that capital punishment is such a good punishment for murder. It must be a greater punishment to the killer's family than to the killer themselves.

l)

> Some murders are more serious than others. For example, murders of police officers should be treated differently from where a husband murders his wife or vice versa.

SAVE AS ...

4 On your own, reread statements a–l and choose the two statements you agree with and the two you disagree with most strongly. Use them to write two paragraphs explaining your own attitude to capital punishment.
5 a) Which of statements a–l could have been said by a Muslim?
   b) Which would definitely not be said by a Muslim?
   Support your answer with evidence from pages 60–61.

How could the Islamic approach to capital punishment help us in Britain today?

E

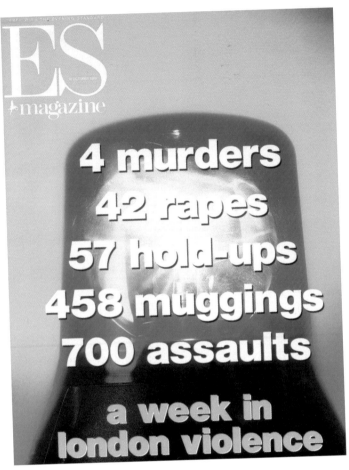

Evening Standard Magazine, 16 October 1998

The British press (who would say they reflect the views of the British people) are often inconsistent in their viewpoint on capital punishment. On the one hand, they pour scorn on the light sentences and easy parole given to killers in Britain. When a particularly horrendous crime is committed, such as serial murder, child killing or terrorist bombing, they say that the punishments for murder are too lenient. On the other hand, they label as 'barbaric' Islamic courts and those of other cultures who sentence people to death.

Crime in Britain is not going away. Source E is simply one indicator of the scale of the problem. Is there anything that Britain could learn from Islamic justice?

FOCUS TASK

Your local MP has been appointed to a special committee in Parliament to look again at whether Britain should reintroduce the death penalty. As a Muslim, you feel that it is important for the committee to consider the Islamic justification for capital punishment.

Write a letter outlining the Islamic teaching on this subject. It should be no longer than one side of A4. These are the topics you will need to cover in your report:

a) The Islamic approach to capital punishment is based on Shari'ah. Shari'ah is …
(You will need to refer back to page 8 and explain why it is viewed as authoritative.)

b) The Qur'an, which is the highest source of authority for Muslims, supports the use of capital punishment in certain cases …
(Explain when and under what conditions the Qur'an allows capital punishment.)

c) Islam teaches that it is very important to be merciful …
(Explain what the compensation option is, and whose right it is.)

d) There are other factors affecting Muslim beliefs about capital punishment …
(Explain how Muslims' beliefs about judgement and life after death affect their ideas about punishment.)

e) Some aspects of the Islamic system of punishment might be useful in Britain …
(Explain your conclusions.)

Issues of life and death – Review tasks

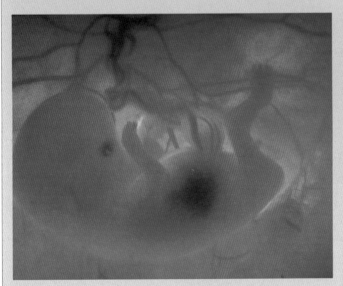

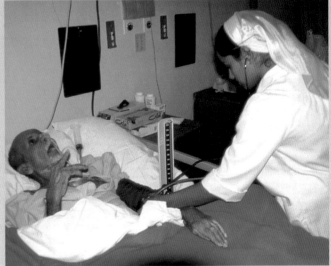

A

1 What name would be given to the deliberate taking of life in each of the pictures on this page?
2 For each one, explain whether Islam would:

- always forbid it
- in some cases forbid it, in others allow it
- always allow individuals to decide.

3 Explain what Muslims believe about:
a) the sanctity of life
b) life after death.
Support each answer with at least two relevant quotations from the Qur'an.

B

'Once you're dead, you're dead. There can be no life after death.'
   Do you agree?
   Give reasons for your answer, showing that you have considered different points of view.

UNIT 4

Relationships

Calligraphy by Salah Al-Moussawy. The text says, 'God supports anyone who supports his brother.' (Prophet Muhammad ﷺ)

Have you ever thought about the number of people with whom you have a relationship? There are probably hundreds, from your close family, through friends, to acquaintances you see only rarely.

What effect do you have on the lives of other people now? What effect will you have in the future?

What kind of a child, sibling, friend, student, acquaintance are you? What kind of a partner, friend, parent could you be? What effect will you have on the lives of your neighbours? What kind of employee or employer will you be?

In this unit you will explore some of these issues. You will be asked to think about your answers to these questions and respond to the way different Muslims might answer them.

4.1 Ummah – the caring community

The united community: Hajj

A

Never have I witnessed such sincere hospitality and overwhelming spirit of true brotherhood as is practised by people of all colours and races here in this ancient Holy Land, the home of Abraham, Muhammad and all the other Prophets of the Holy Scriptures. For the past week, I have been utterly speechless and spellbound by the graciousness I see displayed all around me by people of all colours.

Malcolm X

While I was circling the Ka'bah seven times (TAWAF) all the pilgrims moved together as one ummah; it was impossible to do anything else.

I cannot describe the feeling of praying in a place like this! I am kneeling where Muhammad ﷺ actually stood, fulfilling Allah's commandment.

I am just an ordinary man, but when I come on Hajj I enter the state of IHRAM along with all the other pilgrims. I wear these simple white clothes to symbolise purity, equality and brotherhood of all pilgrims.

At the end of Hajj I, along with the other men here, have my head shaved. This symbolises a new beginning.

When I throw these stones with all the other pilgrims at the pillars that represent Shaytan, I feel that if we stand together we can really fight the evil in the world.

<u>U</u>mmah: what is it?

The words in Source A were spoken by Malcolm X (see pages 94–5) about his experience of Hajj. The Hajj is one of the most dramatic expressions of the Muslim idea of ummah, which means 'community', or 'the worldwide community of Islam'.

Muslims believe that all people were created by Allah with the free will to accept or reject Allah's message. The division into two communities – believers and non-believers – is the only important division among the people of the world. All Muslims therefore belong to one community, united by Allah.

Within this ummah all Muslims are equal whatever their language or nationality. Rich and poor are equal. Men and women are equal.

The Muslim community has a common language, Arabic. All Muslims learn it, even if it is not their main language. Arabic is used to recite the Qur'an, in prayers and in greetings. When Muslims of different racial backgrounds come together to pray, on Hajj or elsewhere, they make the same movements and speak the same words. They are united to other Muslims in their faith in Allah and in their worship.

Of course the ummah is an ideal. It is not easy to achieve and for many Muslims national identity is also strong.

<u>U</u>mmah: who leads it?

In the modern world different branches of Islam have different ideas about day-to-day leadership of the Muslim community (see Checkpoint on page 17). However, they would all agree that Allah is the only ruler of Islam. All Muslims must obey Allah's commands.

<u>U</u>mmah: what is it for?

The aim of the worldwide ummah is to promote the welfare of the whole Muslim community. This is done through the following:

a) supporting other Muslims financially (e.g. zakah and sadaqah, see pages 98–9)
b) encouraging people to live a good life and reject evil ways
c) encouraging people to look after each other.

Two further methods are:

d) DA'WAH – inviting people to Islam by words or by the example of good actions
e) working for unity between Muslim people.

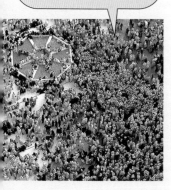

Celebrating this festival of Id-ul-Adha makes me aware of the challenges of being a good Muslim; I must think of others, especially those less fortunate than myself.

ACTIVITY

A school is not an ummah, but it is a community. You are going to explore whether your school community could learn anything from the Muslim ummah.
   Draw up a table like this:

Feature	Purpose	Our school?	Result

a) In the first column, write each feature of the ummah in your own words.
b) In the second column, note how this helps build a sense of community.
c) In the third column, note whether your school also has this feature or anything like it.
d) In the fourth column, note how this feature helps or could help develop your school's sense of community.

The praying community: life at the mosque

✓ CHECKPOINT

The mosque: a place of prayer

'Muhammad 🕮 said, "Wherever the time of prayer overtakes you, pray; that place is a mosque."'

Muslims can, and do, pray anywhere, but they try to pray with other Muslims whenever possible, either in a mosque, or at home or anywhere else, as you can see from the picture on the cover of this book!

The Arabic word for mosque is 'MASJID', which means 'place of prostration'. So the mosque is first and foremost a place for prayer. Several key features of a mosque help in prayer. These are numbered in the picture. Not every mosque in Britain has all of these.

The mosque: a centre of community

Many mosques today as well as being places for prayer have become focal points for the community. They offer support to members of the Muslim community in different ways, as you can see from the picture on this page. This is based on what you might find in a modern, purpose-built, well-equipped mosque.

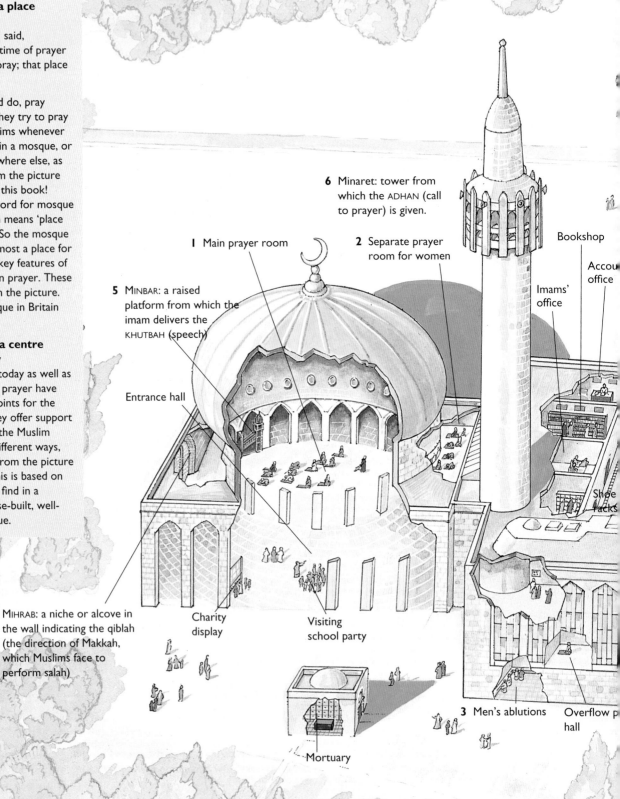

6 Minaret: tower from which the ADHAN (call to prayer) is given.

1 Main prayer room

2 Separate prayer room for women

Bookshop

Accou office

Imams' office

5 MINBAR: a raised platform from which the imam delivers the KHUTBAH (speech)

Entrance hall

Shoe racks

4 MIHRAB: a niche or alcove in the wall indicating the qiblah (the direction of Makkah, which Muslims face to perform salah)

Charity display

Visiting school party

3 Men's ablutions

Overflow p hall

Mortuary

ACTIVITY

1 Make a spider diagram showing the different kinds of activities you can see taking place in this mosque. You might like to group them under the following headings.

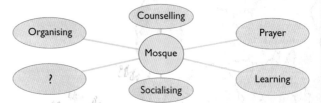

2 Use the information in your spider diagram to design an information sheet to be given to visitors or to be pinned on the mosque notice board. You could target your information sheet at a particular group, e.g. women, men, school parties, etc.

3 An inter-faith meeting is taking place in one of the offices. Why do you think this mosque runs a meeting with members of other religions?

4 Choose three different activities or features from the picture and for each one explain how you think it could help a Muslim to feel part of the Muslim ummah.

5 This is a large well-resourced mosque which provides great support to the local Muslim community. What difficulties would face a Muslim family who lived far away from a mosque like this in an area where there were not many other Muslims?

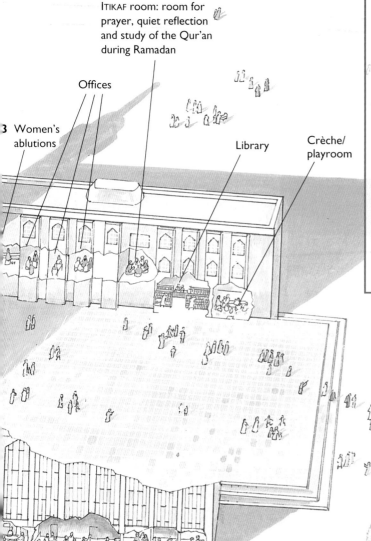

ITIKAF room: room for prayer, quiet reflection and study of the Qur'an during Ramadan

Offices

3 Women's ablutions

Library

Crèche/ playroom

anteen/kitchen

Meeting rooms/ classrooms

The nurturing community: the family

The role of Islam in my family

BIRTH

As soon as possible after a baby is born the adhan (invitation to prayer) is whispered into the baby's ear. This is usually done by the oldest male present. The first word the baby hears is 'Allah'.

MARRIAGE

Muslim families make a great effort to ensure their children have good marriages. All family members attend the weddings of all their relatives and friends.

CHILDHOOD

An important aim of the Muslim family is to give children knowledge and understanding of Islam. This includes learning to recite the Qur'an in its original Arabic.

'Be careful of your duty to Allah and be fair and just to your children.'

Bukhari Hadith

DAILY LIFE

Household and family chores are shared as they are part of every member's duty to the family. Chores also help prepare children for adult life.

LEISURE

Family relationships grow from spending time and having fun together.

OLD AGE

Wherever possible, a Muslim family is expected to care for old and sick relatives at home in the family setting.

'Be kind to your parents, whether one or both of them live to an old age. Do not be rude to them nor send them away, but speak to them in terms of honour.'

Surah 17.23

DEATH

Family members have a responsibility to bury their relatives in the way prescribed by the Hadith. This includes washing the body, dressing it and turning it to face Makkah.

ACTIVITY

1 Draw a timeline like this.

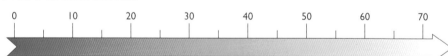

0   10   20   30   40   50   60   70

2 Use the photos and captions to help you to mark on the timeline how a Muslim might be affected by their family at different times in their life.
3 Imagine you have to compile a photo album about your family, or another family you know well.
   a) Make a list of the important events and features of family life you would like to include.
   b) Explain why each is important.
   c) Describe a photograph you would choose to illustrate each feature.

FOCUS TASK

'The world would be a better place if people saw themselves as part of a worldwide community like the ummah.' Do you agree with this statement?

Support your answer with ideas and evidence from pages 66–71. Refer to more than one point of view in your answer.

4.2 Why do Muslims say people should marry?

DISCUSS

It is well known that in Britain today almost one in two marriages will end in divorce, yet marriage is still very popular. Most people will get married at least once in their life. So why do people get married?

In groups:

1 Discuss how you expect your life to be in ten years. Will you be travelling, working, studying? Single, with a partner, married, with children, without children? Close to where you live now, in a different town, county or country? Happy, sad, confused? Lonely, connected?

A

2 Match each cartoon in Source A to one of the ideas in the centre.
3 Why do you think so many people get married? Put the five reasons in Source A in order of importance or add reasons that you think are more important.

SAVE AS ...

4 Write a paragraph to explain which reason you think is most important and why some people may disagree with you.

How do Muslims view marriage?

As you saw from pages 70–71, the family is very important to Muslims. All Muslims are expected to marry. Muhammad ﷺ was married and said, 'He who is able to marry should marry.' (Bukhari Hadith 30.10). Islam teaches that marriage is equally desirable for men and for women. Source B summarises important aspects of Muslim teaching on marriage.

B

1 Sex is a very strong urge. Marriage is the acceptable context in which to express it.	a) *And among His Signs is this: that He created for you mates from among yourselves, that you may live in peace with them.* Surah 30.21
2 Children take many years to become independent. A family gives a secure framework for them to grow up as part of the Muslim community.	b) *A man named Al-Aqra ibn Habis visited the Prophet and was surprised to see him kiss his grandsons, Hasan and Husayn. 'Do you kiss your children?' he asked, adding that he had ten children and never kissed any of them.* *'(That shows) you have no mercy and tenderness at all. Those who do not show mercy to others will not have Allah's mercy shown to them,' commented the noble Prophet.* Hadith
3 Family life teaches people the importance of being kind, affectionate and considerate towards others.	c) *All young people, whoever is able to marry, let him marry, for this will keep him chaste and lower his gaze, and wherever it is not possible let him fast, for surely fasting is going to reduce the sexual drives.* Bukhari Hadith 30.10
4 People need company. Marriage and a family provide companionship.	d) *Be generous, kind and noble to your children and make their habits and manners good and beautiful.* Hadith

---

ACTIVITY

The first column in **Source B** shows reasons why marriage is considered within Islam to be a good thing. The second column contains quotations from the Qur'an and Hadith.

1   Match each reason with one of the quotations.
2   Write a one- or two-word headline to summarise it.
3   Compare the reasons to marry in **Source B** with those in **Source A**. Discuss the similarities and the differences.
4   Why do you think love is not mentioned in **Source B** but sex is?

C

Arranged marriage

Khansa reported, Her father gave her away in marriage ... and she did not like it. So she came to the Messenger of Allah, and he offered to annul the marriage.

Bukhari Hadith 67.43

When the time comes for a young person to get married they usually want their parents' help and support. According to the teachings of Islam, young men and women should not mix freely and so in most Muslim traditions the parents arrange whom their child should marry. This is known as an arranged or introductory marriage.

In all Muslim marriages, parents are expected to have a role in choosing their child's partner. However, as marriage is a contract between individuals, both partners must agree to the match. Muslims are not allowed to arrange a marriage for anybody against their will.

As well as helping their children to choose a suitable marriage partner, Muslim parents also have a responsibility to help if things go wrong. This responsibility may influence their choice.

ACTIVITY

Read the comments below which were made by young Muslims and non-Muslims.

1 My parents know me better than I know myself. They're the best people to choose a partner for me. I know they will choose carefully. They will think about my culture, education, personality and sense of humour and find someone compatible.

2 How can anyone let their parents arrange a marriage for them? The cheek of it. They're not the ones that have to live with the person they've chosen, are they?

3 Just imagine having to marry a woman my parents chose for me! I want to marry someone as different from them as possible!

4 Choosing a partner for myself and taking the consequences of that decision is part of what being an independent adult is all about.

5 To hear people criticise arranged marriages, you would think that in cultures where parents don't arrange the marriage they had no influence at all on their children's choice. That is simply untrue.

6 Having an arranged marriage is not like people say, it's not as if I had to agree to marry the first man my parents suggested.

9 Going out with different people before you choose is good. It helps you learn about yourself, and about what sort of partner you want.

7 Choosing my partner will be one of the most important things in my life. It's very personal. Only I can do it.

8 At least if they arrange the marriage your parents would have to support your partner. My mum just criticises mine!

10 Marriage is a contract between two families as well as two individuals so it makes sense if the rest of the family is involved.

1 Which statements support arranged marriage? Which are against it?

2 Make your own copy of this table. Then use the quotations to complete it. You can add your own ideas as well.

	Advantages	Disadvantages
Marriages based on falling in love with a partner		
Arranged or introductory marriages		

✓ CHECKPOINT

Polygamy

Muslim men are allowed to have up to four wives. At the time of Muhammad ﷺ, it was thought to be the duty of a man to look after as many women as possible. Marriage was the best way to ensure that a woman was secure and treated with respect.

In the Qur'an Allah says,

'Marry women of your choice, two, or three, or four;
But if you fear you will not be able to deal with them fairly.
Then marry only one, or a slave.
That will be suitable to prevent you doing injustice.'

Surah 4.3

Today some scholars say that when a woman is ill or cannot have children a man can take another wife, others say that polygamy is entirely a matter of choice, and others still that polygamy is always wrong because it is impossible to treat more than one wife fairly. A wife may have it written into the marriage contract that she will be the only wife. In Britain, when a husband takes more than one wife, the marriage is recognised by the Shari'ah but not under British law, where bigamy (more than one wife) is illegal.

1 **Look at Source D. Discuss how far the work of a dating agency is similar to or different from the work of parents arranging a marriage for their children.**

2 **Discuss the arguments for and against polygamy. Do you think that this extract from the Qur'an (see Checkpoint) is giving permission for polygamy or guiding people away from it?**

FOCUS TASK

Compile an advice booklet for Muslim parents, to help them explain to their children:

a) why marriage is desirable for Muslims
b) the role of parents in choosing a marriage partner and the reasons for this.

Use the information and sources on pages 72–5 and Source A on page 6.

D

This questionnaire helps Dateline match compatible partners.

E

Anas said,
'Zainab bint Jahsh was
conducted as a bride to
the Prophet 𝕞 and bread
and meat was served, and
I was sent to invite people
to the feast. A party came
and had the meal, then
went out; then another
party came and had the
meal and went out; I went
on thus inviting until I
could not find anyone
whom I should invite.'

Bukhari Hadith 33.8

What happens at a Muslim wedding?

Different Islamic cultures celebrate marriage in different ways. Around the Muslim world different customs are included in Muslim wedding celebrations (see Source F). However, in all cases there is a ceremony which is both religious – with the intention of being witnessed by Allah – and public – in the sight of members of the ummah. Other common features of a Muslim wedding are as follows:

- The marriage is announced.
- A NIKAH (contract) is drawn up. This is agreed between the two families and witnessed by the bride's guardian and two other people.
- A MAHR (marriage gift) is given to the bride by her husband.
- An imam is often present at a wedding ceremony, although this is not required.
- Relevant verses from the Qur'an are usually recited (see Source H).
- A hadith might be told or an informal speech about marriage made.

F

1

A modern-day Muslim wedding in Britain

2

In Sudan we often have an area for the women's celebration and an area for the men's. The wedding usually takes place in the gardens and homes of the families.
At a wedding I feel energetic and happy, and very generous and kind.

A Sudanese Muslim wedding in Britain

3

My parents hired a big hall for my wedding. My cousins spent ages decorating it and making it look beautiful. I was very nervous as I walked into the hall with my father. My husband was there already. We stood on the stage and the imam read some verses from the Qur'an. Then my husband and I were both asked if we agreed to the marriage. We both said yes, of course, but my friends said they couldn't hear me and thought I'd changed my mind!
After the formal part, the party began and we had a wonderful time: there was lots of food and people were very generous with presents. It was the best day of my life.

An imam leads prayers for the bride and groom

G

'I, (name of bride) marry you.'
The groom will say: 'I accept you.'

Example of a marriage announcement

H

In the name of Allah, most Gracious, most Merciful.
O mankind! Be conscious of your Lord and Sustainer
Who created you from a single soul
and from it created its mate
and from them both has spread abroad a multitude of
*   men and women.*
And remain conscious of Allah
in Whom you claim (your rights) of one another,
and of the ties of kinship.
Indeed, Allah is ever watchful over you.

Surah 4.1. An example of a marriage reading

4

Witnessing of the marriage contract

5

In some cultures the bride's hands are decorated with henna and jewellery.

A man's duties towards his wife

- The groom has to give a mahr to the bride. In the Sunni tradition it can be made at the time of the nikah (see opposite) or over a period of time. For Shi'ah Muslims it must be given straight away. The mahr is a form of security stored in case of a future emergency. It is the wife's property and the husband can never claim it back.
- A man must provide for the financial needs of his family. Men are seen as the 'protectors and maintainers' of women (Surah 4.34).
- A man may marry up to four wives, provided he can treat them equally.
- A man must treat his wife and children fairly.
- He must not be involved in sex outside marriage.

A woman's duties towards her husband

- A woman must protect her husband's property in his absence.
- She must be faithful to him.
- She must dress modestly and cover herself when in the presence of people outside the family or when she goes out of the home.
- She must ensure that the home is well managed and that the children are brought up well, even if she works.
- She must obey her husband, as long as he does not ask her to break the laws of Allah.

ACTIVITY

1 **Divide a sheet of paper into four boxes. In each box draw a feature of a typical Muslim wedding. For example, some jewellery could illustrate the mahr. Write a caption underneath explaining why that feature is important.**
2 **Work with a partner. One of you draft a non-religious marriage contract. The other draft a Muslim marriage contract using the text on this page to help you. Each contract should clearly list the responsibilities of each partner.**
3 **Discuss the similarities and differences between the two contracts.**
4 **Would you be prepared to sign either contract yourself? Explain your answer.**

SAVE AS ...

5 **'It is important for religious believers to have a religious wedding.'**
   Do you agree? Refer to Islam in your answer and show that you have considered other points of view.

Sex

It will be clear to you from all that you have studied that Islam is regarded as a complete way of life. Muslims' *belief* in Allah and their feelings of *responsibility* to Allah affect all aspects of life. This applies to even the most intimate areas of life, such as sex. What does Islam have to say about sexual relationships?

Islam teaches that sex is a natural part of human life. The sex drive is natural and God-given. Sex is a gift from Allah.

Muslims believe that Allah has provided perfect guidance about the right way to satisfy these proper needs in an Islamic way: sex must be part of marriage. That way sex leads to peace and avoids extremes of behaviour. Sex outside marriage is absolutely forbidden in the Qur'an.

So, since the sex drive is strong, all Muslims should marry if they can – there is no reward for celibacy. They should marry and they should have

sex: to produce children, for their physical satisfaction and to build a relationship of love and kindness between husband and wife.

Sex satisfies physical needs and emotional needs, but Islam does not see these as separate from spiritual needs. It is a spiritual need to satisfy these other needs in a way acceptable to Allah. One hadith reports Muhammad ﷺ saying that when a husband and wife have sex they are earning rewards in heaven since they have satisfied their needs in a halal way.

There are many other hadith about sex (see Sources I–K for examples). Sex was clearly an issue that concerned some of Muhammad's ﷺ followers since they sought teaching on it. Muhammad ﷺ is regarded as a perfect example of the ideal husband. Some hadith tell us about Muhammad's ﷺ attitude to sex (see Source I). Other hadith talk very frankly about his sex life (see Source J).

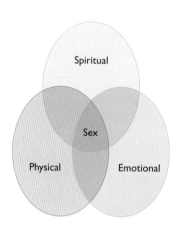

Spiritual

Sex

Physical

Emotional

DISCUSS

Discuss Sources I–K.

1 **What do these sources have to say about:**
   a) **the place of sex within a relationship**
   b) **the importance of sexual hygiene?**
2 **Do you think this advice is valuable for Muslims only or for Muslims and non-Muslims alike?**
3 **Hadith such as I–K are very open in talking about sex, but elsewhere Muhammad ﷺ prohibited Muslims from talking to others about 'intimate relations'. Why do you think there is this contrast?**

I

The Prophet said 'Muslims should not go to their wives like animals but should send a messenger.' When asked what this 'messenger' was, he replied, 'The tender kiss or pleasant talk.'

Bukhari Hadith

J

Narrated Abu Rafi':
One day the Prophet (Peace Be Upon Him) had intercourse with all his wives. He took a bath after each intercourse. I asked him: Apostle of Allah, why don't you make it a single bath? He replied: This is more purifying, better and cleaning.

Abu Dawud Hadith Book I, Number 0219. After his wife Khadijah died Muhammad married a number of wives.

K

It is recorded that a woman complained in the hearing of Umar, the second Khalifah, about the long absence of her husband who had been sent to the battlefield. After consulting his daughter about the length of time a woman could comfortably be without her husband, Umar ordered that four months be the maximum period each soldier could be made to spend at a stretch away from his family.

Hadith

Streetwatch: Balsall Heath

If sex belongs in the intimacy of marriage, how might Muslims respond to others around them who live by different rules? One extreme example of this was the situation faced by the Muslim community of Balsall Heath, Birmingham in 1994.

The issue

The streets of this area – with a high Muslim population – had become the centre of a £10 million-a-year prostitution business. Local women were being approached by kerb-crawlers looking for prostitutes. Some prostitutes had starting soliciting (looking for clients) right outside the mosque.

The Muslim community met to consider their response.

ACTIVITY

In a group, imagine that you are residents of Balsall Heath. Some of you may be Muslims, others not. You have met to consider the problem of the prostitutes and kerb-crawlers in Balsall Heath and to devise a way of dealing with it.

Do a role play of this meeting. Your teacher can give you some possible solutions to consider if you need help.

The response

The residents decided to form a picket on the streets which they called Streetwatch. They put up banners warning the kerb-crawlers that their licence-plate numbers would be taken and given to the police. In a short time, nearly all the prostitutes had stopped working in Balsall Heath and, significantly, the police reported no increase in their activity in neighbouring areas.

In 1995, the Streetwatch programme received official status. The police invited 80 members of the picket to be properly trained as part of a Home Office Streetwatch scheme. When the training was complete, they were given an official ID card.

L

Raja Amin, Chairman of Balsall Heath Streetwatch

Divorce: a case study

Source M is a step-by-step account of a divorce case dealt with by the Islamic Shari'a Council.

M

The characters

Wife: young British woman, married in 1989, whose husband has gone to the USA and failed to contact her for three years. He allegedly went to set up home and make arrangements for her to join him.

Husband: young man claiming US citizenship, whereabouts are unknown. He is allegedly in the USA setting up home for his bride, but has failed to keep regular contact with her or her family.

Wife's family: concerned about the wife and her missing husband. Willing to make strenuous efforts to sort the marriage out in an appropriate way. Her father is particularly concerned and actively involved in trying to resolve his daughter's problems.

Letter 1
Wife's father writes to ISC requesting divorce on grounds of irretrievable breakdown of marriage.

Letter 2
ISC writes to husband asking for 'KHUL (divorce) in exchange for the mahr he gave her.

1992

Letter 3
Wife's father writes to ISC to request divorce on grounds of desertion by the husband. He explains:

- I knew the family of the husband over a period of thirty years
- after the wedding the husband went to California, supposedly to sort out visa and immigration formalities. These were necessary since he was a US citizen and his wife a British subject
- it turns out that the husband has only just received US Alien status and that my daughter has no right to join him immediately
- no maintenance money has been sent to my daughter.

Letter 4
Father writes again to ISC. Husband is missing in the USA.

- Please send information about major Islamic centres in the USA and Canada so I can inform them, with view to stopping husband marrying again.
- I have heard that husband is being unfaithful, although no evidence has been provided.
- My daughter's health is deteriorating.
- We request TALAQ (divorce) from unfaithful husband.

Islamic Shari'a Council
(ISC): set up to solve the marriage problems of Muslims living in Britain in the light of Islamic family law. The Council has members from all the major Muslim groups and schools of thought in the UK. It is widely accepted as an authoritative body with regard to Islamic law.

ACTIVITY

1   Imagine that you work for a helpline for Muslim women in distress. The wife has telephoned you at the time when Letter 4 was written. She tells you of her circumstances. How will you react and what advice will you give? Role play this conversation with a partner.
2   Swap roles and have a conversation at the time of Letter 6.
3   Do you think that having gone so far with divorce proceedings, the wife was right to attempt a reconciliation? Explain why other people might take a different view.
4   It is likely that this marriage was 'arranged'. How did the wife's family continue to take responsibility for the relationship once it had started to break down?

N

If a wife fears abuse or desertion by her husband, it should not be held against either of them if they should try to come to terms; coming to an agreement and preserving the marriage is best while greed is ever present in the [human] soul. Yet if you act kindly and do your duty, Allah will be informed of anything you do.

Surah 4.128

Letter 7
ISC writes to the wife enclosing a divorce certificate.

Letter 6
Father writes to ISC:
Husband took my daughter to the USA and invited us to visit them. He had asked for $10,000 to set up home, which we sent. When my daughter then visited England for her citizenship interview, husband denied any knowledge of her and cancelled his sponsorship of her application. Now neither he nor his family can be traced.

Letter 5
Father writes to ISC:
Husband has suddenly returned to England and attempts at a reconciliation are being made.

August 1993

1994

June 1995

What Islam teaches about divorce

The basic principle for Muslims is that marriage should last until the death of one of the partners. Muslims value family life very highly. An important principle in the divorce process is that marriages should be saved if possible.

O

If you fear a breach between a man and his wife, appoint two arbiters, one from his family and the other from hers. If both want to be brought back together, Allah will settle things between them.

Surah 4.35

P

With Allah the most hateful of the things made lawful is divorce.

Abu Dawood Hadith 13.3

Divorce is a last resort, only to be used when all attempts to save a marriage have failed and the couple are incapable of continuing in a mutual partnership. If that is the case, divorce is allowed.

Men divorcing women

There are several methods of divorce for Muslim men. These practices are interpretations of instructions in the Qur'an which, when they were first revealed to Muhammad 🕌 over 1400 years ago, greatly improved the rights of women. Up to that time, women could be treated like 'worn-out carpets' and divorced at will.

The best way to divorce: allow time for reconciliation
- A husband says 'I divorce you' to his wife. Then there is an IDDAH period, usually of three months, which is designed to allow time for reflection and reconciliation. This also ensures that the wife is not divorced when she is unknowingly pregnant. If the woman is pregnant, the iddah lasts until the woman has recovered from the birth.
- If there is no reconciliation during the iddah period, the couple are divorced. Sexual relations during the iddah count as reconciliation.
- If there has been a reconciliation during the iddah period, the couple are still married. If at any time during the marriage, the husband again divorces the wife, they go through the same waiting process.
- A third pronouncement of divorce is effective immediately. However, the iddah period applies before the wife can marry someone else. They cannot marry each other at any time in the future unless she has been married to someone else in the meantime.

A wrong way to divorce: instant
A husband says 'I divorce you' three times to his wife all at the same time. There are two opinions about such a divorce:

- for most scholars, the couple are now divorced (as in the third divorce above).
- for some scholars, three divorces pronounced at once would be treated as one divorce only. There is an iddah period, with possible reconciliation as above.

In Islam, when a man initiates a divorce he ought to guarantee a woman's rights and dignity. He must return any dowry and make sure her financial obligations are met. The honour of both parties must be maintained and good relations kept with the children. The father is also responsible for any children.

1 'Women shall have rights similar to the rights against them.' (Surah 2.228).
Men can give a divorce, women can apply to be granted one. Do you think that men and women have equal rights in Muslim marriages?

2 What do you think could be the advantages and disadvantages of family members being involved in trying to resolve problems faced by couples?

FOCUS TASK A

A Muslim woman can seek divorce in a number of different circumstances (see below). Make up your own story which explains how events in one of these circumstances might lead to divorce. You will need to show that you understand the different stages of a Muslim divorce. For example, make sure that your story includes efforts at reconciliation before the divorce is final.

You could present your answer in the form of a timeline as on pages 80–81.

Women divorcing men

Divorce by talaq is the right of the husband although the woman can ask for the right to divorce in this way by having it written into her marriage contract at the time it is agreed. Otherwise a woman who wants a divorce can ask for divorce by 'khul, which means she can have her case presented to a Shari'ah court, such as the Islamic Shari'a Council in Britain or another scholarly authority.

Circumstances in which a Muslim woman might seek divorce:

*   adultery
*   desertion
*   lack of companionship or marital relations over four months without any good cause
*   lack of maintenance by her husband
*   harm by her husband
*   insults to herself or her parents
*   breaking any other part of the nikah (marriage contract).

If a woman asks for a divorce and the man is innocent of any fault, she has to agree to give back the mahr (marriage gift) if the husband asks for it. However, if the man has not behaved well towards his wife, the judge may decide that the man is not entitled to anything.

Q

Divorced women shall wait for three monthly periods.
They must not hide what Allah has created in their wombs,
If they have faith in Allah and the Last Day
And their husbands have the better right to take them back
In that period, if they wish for reconciliation.
And women shall have rights similar to the rights against them, according to what is right and fair …
A divorce is only permissible twice:
After that, the parties should either stay together on equitable terms or separate with kindness.
It is not lawful for men to take back any of the marriage gifts you gave your wives.
Except when both parties fear that they would be unable to keep the limits ordained by Allah.

Surah 2.228–9

FOCUS TASK B

You have studied many different aspects of Muslim teaching about sex, marriage, divorce and family life over these 13 pages. It is now time to draw some general conclusions. You are going to write your own answer to the question: 'How do Muslims try to make marriages work?' Write a paragraph on each of the following:

a) why Muslims say people should marry
b) how Muslims try to choose suitable marriage partners for their children and support the couple
c) how the Muslim contracts and ceremonies lay the foundations for the marriage
d) how divorce can work to reconcile Muslim couples
e) your own conclusions: what have you learnt from these measures about your own attitudes to relationships?

4.3 Does Islam truly liberate women?

A

HOW THE OTHER HALF GIVES

OVER THE CENTURIES, WE HAVE GIVEN INSPIRATION, ERUDITION AND COMPASSION TO OUR COMMUNITIES – OUR MEN AND OUR CHILDREN. THE LEAST WE CAN EXPECT IN RETURN IS RECOGNITION. *A SMALL KINDNESS* CHALLENGED SOME BROTHERS TO PROVIDE EXAMPLES, PAST AND PRESENT, OF MUSLIM WOMEN WHO PUT THE 'HER' INTO HISTORY.

I would choose FATIMA because of her power, strength and intelligence.

She had a difficult time, being the daughter of a prophet. She was a collector of hadith, and she had influence over her husband and children, who used to discuss the revelations of the Prophet 🌸 with her. She suffered a great deal throughout her life, and there were many incidents in her life that proved her strength.

A more recent example would be BINT AL-HUDA,

the sister of the Iraqi alim, Muhammad Baqir al-Sadr. Both were imprisoned by Saddam Hussein, but they refused to break under pressure. She was tortured and died as a result.

I admire women who are politically active in the face of opposition and adversity; women who empower themselves and withstand pressure, because I believe women can become leaders despite the fact that it's more difficult for them to attain positions of power. Women have to keep proving themselves (in every society, not just Muslim ones) and men are always opposed to accepting female leaders.

Ahmed Versi, Editor, *Muslim News*

An often ignored example of a steadfast believer is ASIYA, the wife of Pharaoh

who is mentioned in the Qur'an as having beseeched Allah: 'O my Lord! Build for me, in nearness to Thee, a mansion in the Garden, and save me from Pharaoh and his doings, and save me from those that do wrong' (66.11). Her case is one that touched my heart and mind because it shows that she was looking for truth and she failed to find it among the riches and palaces of Pharaoh. She found it with the Master of the worlds: Allah. There is a lesson for us all in this: wealth cannot solve our problems and does not bring happiness but, as Asiya realised, only Allah can provide such things.

Fadi Itani, Manager, *Islamic Relief UK*

Muslim history is full of examples of women who came to prominence for their remarkable sacrifices; one such woman is ASMA BINT ABU-BAKR.

With Prophet Muhammad 🌸 and her father hiding in Hira (on the outskirts of Makkah) away from the city's hatred and hostility, Asma risked her life by undertaking to supply them food and liaise with the outside world. Day by day she journeyed to and fro as a lifeline. Asma was an unknown soldier who assisted in realising the successful process of Islamic da'wah (the spread of Islam).

Dr Mohammed Mahjoub, Publisher

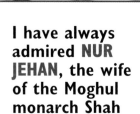

ACTIVITY

Read Source A and explain which of these women you most admire. Give reasons for your choice.

I have always admired NUR JEHAN, the wife of the Moghul monarch Shah Jehan,

because she represents one of the few honest people of power in later Islamic history. She was a great believer in justice for all. The palace of Shah Jehan apparently had a 'chain of justice' which any member of the community could pull to alert the palace that he or she had been wronged. There was a famous incident in which a complaint was brought against Nur Jehan herself. She was accused of causing the death of a washerman. Nur Jehan was willing to submit to the laws of Islamic justice and offered either her life or monetary compensation to the victim's family. Compensation was accepted. Nur Jehan was a classic example of female power behind the throne. She was a source of comfort and wisdom for her husband, and the strength of their attachment is celebrated in one of the greatest feats of architectural excellence: the Taj Mahal.

Muhammad Siddiq Choudry, Retired Mechanical Engineer

From my life, one of the women I have been influenced by is my eldest sister, NASIRA.

Her words of wisdom and encouragement during the aftermath of the partition of India in 1947 forever changed my life. She is the oldest of ten and there is a fifteen-year age gap between us, so she always seemed like a second mother to me. Even when she married and moved away to her husband's household she was always so concerned with our well-being. When the rest of the family was violently up-rooted from our home in India, she was already established in Pakistan and we turned to her for support and stability. She pushed me towards resuming my education and made me understand that there was life outside the provincial world of farming. When the family's fortunes were low, she never failed to provide kindness and encouragement, and for that I will be forever grateful.

I would have to choose my MOTHER,

a doctor, who brought us up single-handedly after the death of our father. Most of all, she has inspired my sister and I with confidence and encouraged us to confront situations head on. She has always taught us to be steadfast in our aims and not to succumb to adverse pressures. My mother has led by example: given that she graduated in Pakistan, she succeeded in a male-dominated environment. Also, the fact that she does so many things at once and all with the same degree of enthusiasm is motivating. But, despite all the pressures she faces, my mother is always there for us, and has always provided the warmth and encouragement we've needed.

Ali Miraj, Accountant

Adapted from *A Small Kindness*, newsletter of the Muslim Women's Helpline (see page 19), Issue 2, April 1997

Addressing the stereotypes

Many Muslims believe that Allah and Muhammad ﷺ set high standards for the treatment of women. Before Islam:

- it was common for Arabs to kill their baby daughters (female infanticide), as they were considered far less useful than sons
- women did not have the right to own property
- women were dependent upon their fathers or their husbands for all their basic human needs, such as food and shelter
- widows and women who had been deserted by their husbands could be left destitute.

The revelations Muhammad ﷺ received in Makkah contained many challenges to these practices. He passed on the message from Allah that women were to have rights to property and that female infanticide should stop. He helped to improve women's status and conditions, and called for people to treat widows and orphans fairly. The Qur'an puts equal religious duties on men and women.

B

For Muslim men and women
For believing men and women
For devout men and women
For true men and women
For men and women who are patient and constant
For men and women who humble themselves
For men and women who give in charity
For men and women who fast and deny themselves
For men and women who guard their chastity and
For men and women who spend time praising God,
For them has God prepared forgiveness and great reward.

Surah 33.35

Ahmed Versi, editor of *Muslim News*, has described Islam as a 'women-friendly' religion. He points to many examples around the world of Islam promoting women's opportunities.

C

… there are countries where Islamic law is implemented where the women are empowered. In Sudan, there are 21 women in the parliament. The Federal Supreme Court, the highest judicial body in Sudan, has three female judges: in the British equivalent body there are none. These women earn the same pay as their male counterparts; a total of 70 women work in the judiciary there.

Nor is there any bar against women obtaining positions of power and serving in government. Professor Sit el Nafar Badi, for example, chairs the Industrial Committee of the National Assembly with 40 men working under her. Yet this is a country where Islamic law is implemented.

So where does the stereotyping of Islam as oppressive to women originate? Why does it receive such attention in the Western media? And why is so little attention given to Islamic countries where women do participate fully in public life?

Ahmed Versi, from Face to Faith, the *Guardian*, March 1997

However, this is not the impression many non-Muslims have of Islam. So let's tackle the stereotypes and look at what Muslims say about some of these issues.

The stereotype says ...

> Muslim women don't get an education because it is a waste of time and money.

> Muslim women are forced to hide their bodies under heavy veils.

> Muslim women stay at home looking after the children.

But by contrast ...

Islam teaches ...

What do you think?

Students studying computing at Gaza University

The **education of women** is considered to be very important in Islam.

D

'Knowledge' for a Muslim is not divided into sacred and secular, and the implications of this in modern terms is that every Muslim, boy or girl, man or woman, should pursue their education as far as possible, bearing in mind the words of the Qur'an:

'Only those of His servants who are learned truly fear Allah'.   Surah 35.28

From Women in Islam by Aisha Lemu and Fatima Heeren

1 Why did Muhammad ﷺ put such emphasis on education for *all* Muslims?
2 What are the effects on society of educating women?
3 What difficulties might a Muslim woman in Britain have in pursuing her education as far as she is able? How might these be overcome?

The principle of **Islamic dress** is modesty.

'Say to the believing men that they should lower their gaze and guard their modesty ... And say to the believing women that they should draw their veils over their bosoms and not display their beauty except to their husbands, and [other close family members].'   Surah 24.3–1

Regarding HIJAB, (veiled clothing), one view is that wearing hijab liberates women. These women are not 'sex-objects' in the eyes of lustful men! Men's appreciation of them is because of their personality, not their appearance. The need for women to dress modestly is as great now as it ever was.

There is discussion among Muslims about whether instructions are to be followed word-for-word or whether it is sufficient to be guided by the principle behind the instruction, i.e. modest dress appropriate to each person's individual circumstances.

Dr Hay Yahan giving a lecture

4 Why, according to the Qur'an, is it appropriate for women to wear hijab when they go out?
5 Why do you think the way Muslim women dress is a controversial issue today?

A Muslim woman is responsible for the care of the home and the welfare of the family, but is allowed to go to **work** and earn her own money.

E

'Women have the same rights in relation to their husbands as are expected in all decency from them; while men stand a step above them.'   Surah 2.228

'I think that this one sentence includes all that is necessary for my happiness as a woman. It grants me all the rights to which I aspire – the right to education, for my property, for being the guardian inside the house and even for a job if circumstances demand it.'

From Women in Islam by Aisha Lemu and Fatima Heeren

Women in Malaysia running a food business in a market

6 What conditions need to be fulfilled if a married Muslim woman is to work?
7 Women sometimes experience discrimination in the workplace. How might a Muslim woman, in particular, experience discrimination at work?
8 How might she deal with it?

F

MOTHERS IN ISLAM

'... *Reverence Allah through Whom you demand your mutual rights and reverence the wombs (that bore you) for Allah ever watches over you.'* (Surah 4.1)

Exalted

The meaning of Allah's words in the Qur'an reflect the exalted position that a mother occupies in Islam. She is mentioned in the same verse as the most important duty of a Muslim – that of worshipping, respecting and obeying Allah the Almighty. This reflects the high standing of a mother in Allah's sight, and indicates how valuable a mother's role and personality are.

However, many women nowadays, including Muslim women, feel that motherhood is unrewarding or not essential. It is not considered to be a career that brings in financial reward and constant fulfilment! How wrong they are!

High-flying

Allah the Most High has filled the life of a mother with opportunities, challenges, immense reward and constant fulfilment! Further, a mother carries out the tasks of many high-flying professionals! She is her child's carer, comforter, provider, supporter, teacher, doctor, guardian, protector, rewarder, playmate, best friend and much, much more. Her role is varied, rewarding

and indispensable, more so than any other that is on offer! A mother does her duty in an environment of care, love and respect whereas many women are victims of harassment in their workplaces! Despite this, women continue to claim to be happier in their jobs than being mothers!

A noble profession

A mother uniquely is entrusted with the noble task of guiding and teaching, training and enriching the future generation which begins with her child. Motherhood is itself a noble profession. It requires skill and professionalism, commitment and care, devotion and dedication. This is why Allah Most Kind instructs a mother to concentrate on shaping the future generation first, before pursuing a career outside parenting if she wishes. A woman will not experience the same satisfaction or

reward, love or honour in general employment as she will as a mother in her family circle.

Worship

To bring up and care for a child is one of the greatest forms of ibadah (worship) that a woman undertakes in Islam. If only we were to realise the immense rewards and blessing contained in motherhood, both in this life and the Hereafter, then all women would be yearning to become mothers! She is rewarded for every hardship suffered and every happiness experienced while bringing up her child. Then when her child reaches maturity and engages in upright conduct – the result of mother's teachings – again the mother is rewarded for all this. Even when the mother's life has ended and her soul has departed, she continues to benefit, since her righteous child will continuously pray for the mother's forgiveness.

Honoured servants

O Muslim! We must realise that success and fulfilment lie at the door of our respected mothers; let us value them and love them, honour them and always aid them; they live for us! They give up the world for us! How can we re-pay them for their kindness? And know, dear reader, that it is through these honoured servants, our mothers, that the rest of us have the promise of salvation and ease. The Prophet ﷺ said: 'Paradise lies at the feet of your mother.' (Hadith)

1 According to this article, what qualities are expected of a good mother?
2 Which three qualities do you think are most important? Why?
3 Can men have these qualities? Explain your answer.
4 Do you agree with Ayesha Bint Mahmood's view on the value of motherhood?
   Write a letter to *Trends* magazine to explain your view. You should show that you have considered other points of view. You might want to refer to Source E on page 87 in your letter.

From an article by Ayesha Bint Mahmood in *Trends*

4.4 How do Muslims respond to racism?

✓ CHECKPOINT

Prejudice and discrimination

• PREJUDICE is an attitude. It means having an opinion which is not based on fact.

• DISCRIMINATION is an action. It means treating someone unfairly because of your prejudice.

The law

In Britain, the Race Relations Act (1976) makes it unlawful to discriminate against anyone on grounds of race, colour, nationality or ethnic origin. It gives people the right to claim compensation for discrimination, harassment and victimisation. It applies to jobs, training, housing, education and the provision of goods, facilities and services.

Racial violence and other racial incidents are offences under criminal law. Inciting racial hatred is also a criminal offence. However, racial prejudice is not against the law, because an attitude cannot be made illegal.

What are Racial Equality Councils?

The government's Commission for Racial Equality helps to fund a number of Racial Equality Councils (RECs). These are organisations that work in local areas, among local communities, to promote racial equality and tackle racial discrimination. There are currently 108 RECs and similar organisations.

Islamophobia

Maqsood Ahmad has been the director of the Kirklees Racial Equality Council since 1994. We asked him about his work and the work of the Commission on British Muslims and Islamophobia set up by the Runnymede Trust.

> The term 'Islamophobia' is used to refer to dread or hatred of Islam and of Muslims. It can be found in all forms of media and in all sections of society. It affects the lives of Muslims of all ethnic backgrounds; it is not the same as racism.

> The Kirklees Racial Equality Council carried out a two-week survey into the way different religious groups are portrayed in daily newspapers in Britain. It confirmed our view that the press is Islamophobic.

ACTIVITY

In groups, you are going to carry out your own small-scale research using the same methods as Kirklees REC. Your group will need a selection of local and national tabloid and broadsheet newspapers.

1   Look for references to any religion and record whether the religion is portrayed in a positive, neutral or negative light. Use a table like the one below to help you. Keep the references, as you will need them to answer question 2 on page 90.

Religion	Newspaper, date and page number	Summary	Portrayal	Reason
Islam	The Daily News, 14 February 1999, page 2	A Muslim man who rescues a drowning dog	Positive	Man described as a 'kindly Muslim'

2   When everyone has found at least one reference collect your group's evidence in a table like the one below:

Religion	Number of positive references	Number of neutral references	Number of negative references

3   Collect each group's totals in a large table and discuss the results.

The Runnymede Commission on British Muslims

In 1997 a report called 'Islamophobia – a challenge for us all' by the Runnymede Commission on British Muslims and Islamophobia was published. I was a member of this multi-ethnic and multi-religious committee, which included some people who had considerable experience of community relations and religious affairs. The members visited areas where many Muslims live and received reports and letters from groups and individuals around the country, Muslim and non-Muslim.

The key questions asked by the members of the commission were probably very similar to those you are asking:
- What is Islamophobia?
- What are the effects of Islamophobia?
- Can the law help?
- What else can be done?

The first main point made in the report was that:

Closed views of Islam are a key feature of Islamophobia.

If you have a *closed* view of something, your attitude is not based on reason or logic. It is your view and you are going to stick to it, even if someone proves logically that you are wrong. In a phobia, the attitude is one of fear.

If you have an *open* view of something, you are prepared to change that view as a result of debate and discussion or if there is evidence that you were wrong.

A

Closed view: Islam is ...	Open view: Islam is ...
1 Indivisible, rigid set of ideas	Diverse and forward-looking
2 Separate: **(a)** not having any aims or values in common with other cultures **(b)** not being affected by them **(c)** not having any influence over them	Interacting: involved in a dialogue with other faiths and cultures **(a)** having certain shared values and aims **(b)** affected by them **(c)** having a positive effect on them
3 Inferior to the West	Distinctively different, but not deficient
4 Enemy: violent, aggressive, threatening, supportive of terrorism	Partner in co-operative projects and in the solution of shared problems
5 Manipulative: a political set of ideals, used to gain political or military advantage	A genuine religious faith practised sincerely by Muslims
6 Any criticism Islam makes of 'the West' rejected automatically	Any criticism Islam makes of 'the West' considered and debated
7 Dislike of Islam used to justify discrimination against Muslims	Discrimination criticised
8 Islamophobia seen as natural	Islamophobia seen as a problem

Adapted from *Islamophobia – a challenge for us all*

When Muslims are portrayed in the media, you see African Muslims, black Muslims from America, Asian Muslims from Pakistan, India and Iran, but rarely white Muslims. The reporting of the Runnymede Report is a classic example; the media knew that there were many white Muslims who were born here, educated here, were well qualified to discuss the issues, but they didn't go to them.

1 Do you feel that *your* attitude towards Islam is open or closed?
2 As a class, find examples of open and closed views of Islam in the newspaper references you studied in the Activity on page 89.

ACTIVITY A

1 Make your own large copy of Diagram **B** in the centre of an **A3** sheet of paper, leaving plenty of room in the circles.

2 Decide where on your diagram each of the following examples should go.

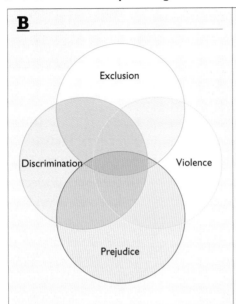

B

Exclusion

Discrimination

Violence

Prejudice

Examples:

- Muslims are refused permission to set up an Islamic voluntary-aided school, even though there are many Jewish and Christian ones

- an employer is inflexible about using annual leave at the time of a religious festival, even though the needs of Christians are met

- tasteless anti-Muslim jokes are made

- there is little effort to understand the religious needs of Muslim hospital patients, e.g. diet

- a mosque is daubed with anti-Muslim slogans

- a Muslim student is forbidden to wear veiled clothing at school

3 With a partner, think of other examples of Islamophobia and place them on your chart. You could get more ideas from pages 92–3.

ACTIVITY B

Source **C** contains some important ideas, but in difficult language. Imagine you have been asked to express this vision as a poster or series of posters for the schools in your area. Work in groups.

1 Each person take one point and sum it up in a short slogan or headline.

2 Either put them all on a single group poster or make up your own poster to illustrate your point.

SAVE AS ...

3 Look at Source **C** again. On a scale of 1 (very unlikely) to 5 (almost certain), say whether you think each of the eight ideas is likely or unlikely to be achieved in the next ten years.

4 Choose one idea which you think is most likely and one which you think is least likely to be achieved and explain your choice.

C

Our vision

1 *Islamophobic discourse will be recognised as unacceptable and will no longer be tolerated in public. Whenever it occurs people in positions of leadership and influence will speak out and condemn it.*

2 *Legal sanctions against religious discrimination, violence and incitement to hatred will be on the statute book.*

3 *British Muslims will participate fully and confidently at all levels in the political, cultural, social and economic life of the country.*

4 *The voices of British Muslims will be fully heard and held in the same respect as the voices of other communities and groups. Their individual and collective contributions to wider society will be acknowledged and celebrated.*

5 *The state system of education will include a number of Muslim schools, and all mainstream state schools will provide effectively for the pastoral, religious and cultural needs of their Muslim pupils. The academic attainment of Muslim pupils will be on a par with that of other pupils.*

6 *The need of young British Muslims to develop their religious and cultural identity in a British context will be accepted and supported.*

7 *Measures to tackle social and economic deprivation, unemployment and urban decline will be of benefit to Muslims as to all other communities.*

8 *All employers and service providers will ensure that, in addition to compliance with legal requirements on non-discrimination, they demonstrate high value for religious, cultural and ethnic diversity.*

The Runnymede Commission published 60 recommendations. The possible impact of these recommendations can be seen in this 'vision for the future'.

Responding to racism

Case study 1: Maqsood Ahmad, Director of Kirklees Racial Equality Council

A Early memories

My earliest memories of racism are from school in Rochdale, where I grew up; I remember people not sitting next to me, throwing things, and calling names. There were only two or three Asians in my class. Young people then just accepted it; got on as best they could. The teachers saw it as children playing pranks. Then you started missing lessons because you were frightened to go into the classroom, so you'd get into trouble with the teachers. It was a hostile environment for people like me. Even outside school you couldn't really get away from it. My mother wouldn't let me play football outside; she wanted to protect me, but you end up excluded from society. It's sad for a British person to be subjected to that type of experience.

B Names and identity

Young Muslims often don't feel positive about their identity; strong role models are important. Whether you are Christian or Muslim or Sikh, you need your own identity. British Muslims also feel they are not protected by legislation, as we are not a racial group and there isn't a religious discrimination act. The government could make Muslims a racial group, or adopt the religious discrimination act from Ireland. Some Muslims are victims of prejudice purely on the grounds of their faith, not because of their colour. That's why a lot of young people today shorten their names, from Mohammed to Mo, Sohail to So, and so on.

I used to be a designer. At first, I called myself Maq. Once my father came to drop my keys off, but the receptionist said, 'Nobody called Maqsood Ahmad works here.' At home I explained, 'They know me as Maq.' He was so disappointed. He said, 'We've given you a very positive name that means "the one who has an aim, who is clear," and Ahmad means "trustworthy", it's a name of the Prophet.' It got me thinking that I knew everybody else's name at work. So I started using my full name and people were amazed by it. 'Maqsood Ahmad, who's this? Pakis work here all of a sudden?' It was interesting to see the reaction, but to challenge it was very, very hard.

C Why I got into anti-racism

I was happy as a designer, but I realised I couldn't get away from racism. You get your windows smashed, dog dirt through your letterbox, your mother is spat at when she goes to the shops, your sister is sworn at and her headscarf is pulled off. It all made me very angry. Only the good sense of my mother and father made me see that not every white person is racist. That's why I got into working against racism.

The first case that came to me as director of Kirklees REC was a young Muslim woman with an Asian background, who was being harassed at her college: she was challenged about everything that Saddam Hussein was doing; students who knew she was fasting kept offering her food, even though she had explained it to them. That is a form of oppression and it affects that person.

If you are attacked on a regular basis, the perpetrators get more and more confident and it wears you down emotionally. Every time you meet someone you wonder, 'Are they treating me differently?' Even if they are not, you are suspicious because of your experience. If my parents hadn't kept talking to me about these issues, I think I'd have ended up hating white people; it's a common reaction. That is why in Kirklees the white community gets the second-largest number of racial attacks.

D Challenging racism

Racist organisations like the National Front were very active in Rochdale when I was growing up. These organisations always breed in areas where they can get support. If no action is taken, it becomes a confident environment for them. But in areas where communities are strong, with good anti-racist activists and a good police force that will take strong action and root these individuals out, others don't express these views. Racist organisations don't cease to exist, but it becomes a hostile area for them.

E Why segregation matters

Rochdale now is highly **segregated**: you have white areas and Asian areas and black areas. So racism is still there. Gangs don't attack the Asian community any more; [Asians] have their own gangs now. I think that's sad. I don't believe the majority of Muslims, Asians and black people want to live apart, I don't think it's healthy, but racism has made us isolated, and we're not the ones moving out. If people stayed and tackled the racism they could build communities with better understanding. I wouldn't say the segregation is an improvement.

The local authority should be asking why people are moving out. Schools should be tackling racism.

ACTIVITY

Work in groups. Read each extract from the interview with Maqsood Ahmad carefully before tackling this task.

Maqsood describes many possible responses to racism.

- fighting back
- action by the local authority
- action by school
- finding and asserting your own identity
- being guided by your religion
- participation in decision-making groups, for example school governing bodies
- segregation
- action by the police
- parents and children talking about the issues
- creating positive role models
- education
- legislation

1 Write each response on a separate card.
2 Write 'Maqsood Ahmad' in one corner of a sheet of A3 paper. Place the response cards according to how you think he feels about each response. Put the ones he would encourage close to him, and the ones he would discourage further away.
3 Now write your name in another corner. Place the cards according to how important *you* would say each response is in solving the problem.

SAVE AS …

4 Write a paragraph to explain how you think being a Muslim has contributed to Maqsood Ahmad's struggle against racism.

F Working with others

I have four children; three daughters and a son. They go to a school which is 40 per cent Muslim, and I am a governor of the school. I think it is important for white parents to see that we don't just care about Muslim children, we care about all children. Sometimes, though, I become frustrated: three or four years ago Asian parents were not coming forward to stand as governors. We ended up going knocking on doors to encourage them.

G The effects of Islam

I think being a Muslim has an influence. Islam doesn't talk about colour or where a person is from. It talks about people. Islam has given me focus. I think young people with a positive identity don't feel a need to put other people down. I know Islam taught me what was wrong and kept me on the right path.

I know **I am accountable for my actions** and will go to heaven or to hell. I don't want when I die to be asked the question 'Why did you treat this person this way?' and have no answer to give. There is a price to pay for treating people badly. People who understand Islam know this. Islam gives me control, as I mustn't put drugs or alcohol into my body. If you are not in control, there is a danger you will do something that you will regret. As a magistrate, I see many people who blame alcohol, blame drugs when they beat their wife or their children. If you keep beating your wife when you are drunk, then perhaps you should stop drinking. If you keep hating people because of the colour of their skin, we can't keep giving you community service.

My favourite stories from Islam tell how the Prophet ﷺ treated other people. He made treaties with his enemies. The first condition was that no child or woman should be hurt. There were rules and regulations even then.

The way Muhammad ﷺ lived is always an inspiration for me. He and the Khalifahs who followed him always lived in the same area as the poorest people. In those areas you are always aware that you have to change and the area has got to change. That constant reminder keeps my commitment to equality very much alive. Unless you are from an area, you can't relate to the tensions of that area. I find more and more often that senior decision-makers in local authorities cannot relate to the racial tensions or the concerns of working-class people. Yet they are the ones making decisions on their behalf.

✓ CHECKPOINT
Equality

You will have heard 'equality' mentioned many times already in your study of Islam. It is a key principle running through the religion, beginning with the account of the creation of humankind: the Qur'an speaks of a multitude of men and women being created from a single soul (Surah 4.1). That people vary in colour and speak different languages is a sign of the power of Allah (Surah 30.22).

The meaning of this teaching is stated in the address Muhammad 靈 gave on his last pilgrimage:

'All of you descend from Adam and Adam was made of earth. There is no superiority for an Arab over a non-Arab nor for a non-Arab over an Arab, neither for a white man over a black man nor a black man over a white man except the superiority gained through consciousness of God (taqwa). Indeed the noblest among you is the one who is most deeply conscious of God.'

When Muhammad 靈 came to Madinah (see page 111), tribal rivalry was making peaceful life impossible.

The 'Constitution of Madinah' established the basic principle that all Muslims are Muslims first and members of any tribe or racial group second. All are equal in the sight of Allah and should treat each other as members of one community – ummah.

Case study 2: Malcolm X

Despite his experiences of racism, Maqsood Ahmad found that his faith, and the careful guidance of his Muslim parents, prevented him from becoming a racist himself. But it would be foolish to think that people who call themselves Muslims can never themselves be guilty of racial prejudice or discrimination.

Malcolm X was one such person. Many of you will have heard of him; you may have even seen the film about his life. He called himself a Muslim for 12 years before he discovered that his own racist views were incompatible with Islam. His story is a tragic one, but also one of hope.

D

Born Malcolm Little in Omaha, Nebraska, north-western USA. Later changed his name to Malcolm X because he believed that Little had been the surname of a white slave-owner; X stood for his unknown African name.

In childhood, developed intense hatred of the white race from seeing how black people were treated and how the Ku Klux Klan harassed his father, Earl Little, a Baptist minister.

Malcolm left school, education incomplete, dreams shattered. Aged 15, he got involved with a dangerous group of friends. Before long he was carrying a gun, stealing and selling drugs.

1925   1931   1940

Aged six, Malcolm found his father deliberately run over by a tram, his skull crushed. Soon after, his mother was declared mentally ill. The children were sent to live with different families.

With his 'new' family, Malcolm started to enjoy high school which, unlike some, was multi-cultural. He was popular and achieved good grades until he began to realise the full implications of the lack of equality between black and white people, the norm in the USA at that time. When Malcolm said he'd like to be a lawyer, his teacher laughed; successful blacks were waiters, caretakers and shoeshine boys then.

E

I have been blessed to visit the Holy City of Makkah. There were tens of thousands of pilgrims, from all over the world. They were of all colours, from blue-eyed blondes to black-skinned Africans. But we were all participating in the same ritual, displaying a spirit of unity and brotherhood that my experiences in America had led me to believe never could exist between the white and non-white.

America needs to understand Islam, because this is the one religion that erases from its society the race problem. Throughout my travels in the Muslim world, I have met, talked to, and even eaten with people who in America would have been considered white – but the white attitude was removed from their minds by the religion of Islam. I have never before seen sincere and true brotherhood practised by all colours together, irrespective of their colour.

FOCUS TASK

Maqsood Ahmad and Malcolm X both experienced racism, but they responded in very different ways. Discuss how the following factors influenced their responses:

- **their experiences of racism**
- **their parents**
- **education**
- **other people**
- **the history of their racial group**
- **Islam.**

June Formed the Organisation of Afro-American Unity. Publicly declared that he was not a racist, and that he had been wrong to make generalisations about the white race.

Left the Nation of Islam.
April Malcolm X made his Hajj to Makkah. Dramatic effect on him and his attitude to people of different races, especially to white people. He changed his name to Al-Hajj Malik El-Shabazz and, as a letter he wrote while on Hajj shows, a much more profound change had come over him (see Source E).

Released from prison, Malcolm gave all his time to the Nation of Islam. He encouraged violence against white people (he called them 'white devils') as the way to end inequality. He had, in effect, become a racist.

| 1946 | 1952 | 1961 | 1964 | 1965 |

Caught robbing a jewellery shop, Malcolm was sentenced to eight years in prison, where he completed his education and joined the Nation of Islam, an offshoot of Islam.

Became disillusioned with the immoral behaviour of the leader of the Nation of Islam.

February 21 Malcolm X was assassinated by black Muslims.

You may be shocked by these words coming from me. But on this pilgrimage, what I have seen, and experienced, has forced me to rearrange much of my thought-patterns previously held, and to toss aside some of my previous conclusions.

During the past eleven days here in the Muslim world, I have eaten from the same plate, drunk from the same glass, and slept on the same rug – while praying to the same God – with fellow Muslims, whose eyes were the bluest of blue, whose hair was the blondest of blond, and whose skin was the whitest of white. And in the words and in the deeds of the white Muslims, I felt the same sincerity that I felt among the black African Muslims of Nigeria, Sudan and Ghana.

We were truly all the same (brothers) – because their belief in one God had removed the white from their minds, the white from their behaviour, and the white from their attitude.

I could see from this, that perhaps if white Americans could accept the Oneness of God, then perhaps, too, they could accept in reality the Oneness of Man – and cease to measure, and hinder, and harm others in terms of their 'differences' in colour.

All praise is due to Allah, the Lord of all the Worlds.

Sincerely,
Al-Hajj Malik El-Shabazz
(Malcolm X)

1 **From the biographical details in Source D, identify the experiences in Malcolm's life that contributed to his developing racist views against white people.**
2 **Use Source E to identify the experiences on the Hajj that caused him to reassess his attitudes.**

From *The Autobiography of Malcolm X*, with assistance from Alex Haley

Relationships – Review tasks

A

CHERRY TREE COLLEGE

Counsellor, with specific responsibility for Muslim students

The college offers a wide range of full- and part-time courses for approximately 5000 post-16 students. As counsellor for Muslim students you will be responsible for providing one-to-one emotional, practical and educational support for these students.

You must be a practising Muslim and be able to give sound advice based on Islamic teaching.

You will have a counselling qualification, at least three years experience and the ability to work under pressure. Please send CV with details of current salary by 15 March.

This task requires you to work on your own and then with one other person.

1 You are a student representative on the council of the college which has advertised this vacancy. The college has a great many Muslim students. It is important that the counsellor:

   • understands the range of issues facing young people in Britain today, e.g. sex, relationships, loneliness, prejudice and discrimination
   • can give 'sound advice based on Islamic teaching'.

   Suggest some questions that could be used to help select an appropriate candidate for this position.

2 With a partner, role play the interview with one candidate. Record the answers, or take notes if this is not possible.

3 Review the answers and decide together which three questions elicited the best answers. Write up these answers and explain whether you would recommend this candidate and why.

B

The couple in this photograph have had an arranged marriage

1 Explain the meaning of the term 'arranged marriage'.
2 State one teaching from the Qur'an that tells Muslims that they are expected to marry.
3 Give three practical examples to show how the practices and teachings of Islam aim to help marriages succeed.
4 'There would be far fewer divorces in Britain if everyone followed the Islamic model.'
   Do you agree or disagree with this statement? Give reasons to support your answer, showing that you have thought about more than one point of view. You must refer to Islam in your answer.

C

1 Explain, with examples, the difference between prejudice and discrimination.
2 Write a paragraph describing how Islam caused Malcolm X to change his views on race.
3 'The teachings of religions make racism worse, not better, because they emphasise the differences between people.'
   Do you agree or disagree with this view? Give reasons to support your answer, showing that you have thought about more than one point of view. You must refer to Islam in your answer.

UNIT 5

Global issues

Address yourself therefore steadfastly to the true faith

The primal pattern out of which Allah originated humankind

There is no changing Allah's creation

That is the exact religion

But most people do not know

Islamic Foundation for Ecology & Environmental Sciences

This is the front cover of a brochure of the Islamic Foundation for Ecology and Environmental Sciences. The quotation is from Surah 30.30.

Over the next twenty pages, you will be investigating some big issues: poverty, the environment, war and peace. Here are some even bigger questions to think about before you start.

Do you feel that the Earth belongs:
- to you
  - to someone else
    - to no one
      - to Allah?

Do you feel that solving the major global problems is:
- your responsibility
  - other people's responsibility
    - Allah's responsibility?

Do you feel the biggest threat to life on Earth is:
- poverty
  - environmental change
    - war
      - something else?

If someone said to you that religion can help solve the Earth's problems, would you:
- agree
  - disagree
    - scream?

5.1   How should Muslims use their money?

A

You will not attain piety until you give what is dear to you.

Surah 3.92

B

to support converts to Islam
to pay for community workers who collect zakah
to relieve people from debt
£1
to educate people about Islam
to look after refugees or stranded travellers
to help poor members of your own community
to ransom hostages or prisoners of war

1 **Sadaqah can be used to help anyone in need. In pairs brainstorm as many kinds of need as you can think of. For each one, decide what form of sadaqah would be most appropriate and give an example of how it would help.**

2 **Explain what Muslims mean when they say:**
   a) zakah is a form of ibadah (worship)
   b) zakah is a purification
   c) zakah is a test.

Read Source D.

3 **List all the different types of people Allah wants Muslims to help.**

4 **List all the reasons given for helping.**

How to give and why to give

Muslims are expected to be generous, kind and compassionate. They have a duty to care for the poor and for those in need. The Qur'an teaches that all human beings are special creations of Allah. Muslims carry out Allah's work on Earth to provide for all people. All wealth actually belongs to Allah.

Muslims differ in how they give and who they give to, but they are all commanded by Allah to give and to give generously. There are three main forms of giving.

Sadaqah

Sadaqah is any good deed that is done for the sake of Allah, rather than for selfish reasons. Sadaqah can be practised at any time and in any place. It may involve a Muslim giving their time, their talents, their money or their prayer. It can even be something small like a smile or picking up a piece of litter. Sadaqah can be given to Muslims or to non-Muslims. It can be given after a person's death through their will.

Zakah

Zakah is the third pillar of Islam (see page 13). All Muslims worldwide who have a certain level of wealth must give a percentage of their savings once a year as zakah to help the poor and needy. Zakah is sometimes called a tax, but it is really an act of ibadah (worship). In the UK, most Muslims pay their zakah by placing it in a collection box in their local mosque. A committee then decides how it should be spent.

Zakah is for the benefit of the poor. In Source B you can see the ways in which zakah may be spent. It cannot be spent on mosques as these belong to the community; that would be like giving it to yourself.

Zakah is 2.5 per cent of savings each year, but other types of wealth attract a higher rate. For example, the rate of zakah on agricultural produce would be 20 per cent. Zakah is collected only on savings. It should not take money away from what a Muslim needs to look after their family, the first priority. The more wealthy a person is, the more they give. One aim of zakah is to transfer money from rich to poor, and so reduce inequality. It encourages Muslims to use their money to create jobs or help others rather than accumulating wealth. If everyone paid zakah, saving would be gradually eroded. Allah wants his followers to resist the temptations of accumulating wealth.

It is not only the recipients who benefit from zakah. The giver does too. Literally the word 'zakah' means 'growth' or 'purification'. Zakah purges the giver of greed and selfishness. It is a form of worship because Allah can be worshipped through giving to people who are part of Allah's creation. Zakah is a test of the Muslim. Wealth belongs to Allah. To spend zakah on oneself would be stealing from Allah. It must be given every year, whether the believer feels like it or not.

Zakat-ul-Fitr

This is an additional payment at the end of Ramadan. The fourth pillar of Islam is to fast during the month of Ramadan (see page 13). Many Muslims say that it is in Ramadan that they most learn to identify with the poor.

The month-long fast ends with the festival of ID-UL-FITR. At this time Muslims are expected to give generously to those in need. These gifts are called ZAKAT-UL-FITR. The rate of this donation is usually suggested by the local mosque and represents the cost of a meal for each member of the donor's family.

C

TIME

PRAYER

A Muslim Aid volunteer programme provides meals for orphans in Bangladesh.

A Turkish Muslim praying to Allah.

SADAQAH IS GIVING ...

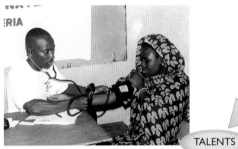

A doctor in Liberia checks a patient's blood pressure in a free clinic.

TALENTS

MONEY

A British businessman donates funds to Muslim Aid's Kosava fund.

Forms of Sadaqah

D

1
He is not a believer who eats while his neighbour remains hungry by his side.

2
If anyone strokes an orphan's head, doing so only for Allah's sake, he will have blessings for every hair over which his hand passes.

3
The Prophet ﷺ said:
The man who exerts himself on behalf of the widow and the poor one is like the one who struggles in the way of Allah, or the one who keeps awake in the night (for prayers) and fasts during the day.'

4
The Prophet Muhammad ﷺ said:
'Every single day, each person has two angels near him who have descended from heaven. The one says, "O Allah, compensate the person who gives to charity," the other says, "O Allah, inflict a loss on the person who withholds his money."'

5
The deeds most loved by Allah are those that are done regularly even though they may be small.

1 Hadith; **2** Prophet Muhammad, in Abu Umamah, Mishkat Al-Masabih 4974; **3** Bukhari Hadith 69.1; **4** Hadith; **5** Bukhari Hadith 76.472

Muslim Aid
WORKING FOR PEOPLE

E   *M*uslim Aid

> Since Muslim Aid's humble beginning [in 1985], we have tried to fulfil the mission of bringing help and assistance to the world's poorest communities and those struck by disaster throughout Africa, Asia and Europe. This has been achieved through the continued support of those who see Muslim Aid as their arms stretching out to assist their brothers and sisters in need.

Yusuf Islam, Chairman of Muslim Aid (1985–93), in Muslim Aid Annual Report 1995

Muslim Aid is an international relief and development agency working to alleviate suffering among the world's poorest and most needy communities. Set up in 1985 by leading British Muslim organisations, it supports projects in 44 of the poorest countries in Africa, Asia and Europe.

Muslim Aid has field offices in Bangladesh, Somalia and Sudan, sister branches in Australia and Germany and over 200 partner organisations in the poor countries. It receives voluntary contributions from individuals, businesses and organisations in the form of zakah, sadaqah, legacies and other charitable giving. In 1998, it raised about £2.5 million to help the poor.

How does Muslim Aid spend its money?

Muslim Aid responds quickly to emergencies by sending relief supplies such as food, medicine and clothes to the victims of natural disaster, war and famine. However, like most overseas charities, its most important work is to tackle the root causes of poverty by funding long-term development projects. The programmes include the provision of safe clean water, healthcare, skills training, education and welfare for the most vulnerable sections of the society such as orphans and widows. The aim of the development work is that the people are able to help themselves.

Although the beneficiaries are mostly Muslim, Muslim Aid helps the poor and the needy regardless of race, ethnicity, colour or religion.

F

Helping the victims of natural disaster

In 1998, terrible floods devastated the lives of 30 million people in Bangladesh. Diseases such as malaria, typhoid and dysentery spread due to contaminated water. Muslim Aid launched a large-scale appeal and provided more than £350,000 to help people rebuild houses and install thousands of hand-pumps for safe, clean water. It supplied aid packages containing food, medicine and clothing. Boats were used to reach the most needy and isolated communities.

Education and skills training

In Sudan, Muslim Aid helped to train more than 2,200 women in typing, tailoring, handicrafts and computer skills, and over 900 young people in literacy, woodwork, leatherwork and electronics. In the Eddain displaced persons camp in South Darfur, it spent £15,000 providing education to 1,724 needy children.

Mohammed Ashraf: a Muslim Aid volunteer

Mohammed Ashraf has been a regular Muslim Aid donor since 1985. Ten years ago, he underwent major heart surgery and was forced to leave his job as a metal finisher. Though registered disabled and 69 years old, he has found a new lease of life as a Muslim Aid volunteer. He has collected over £20,000 in donations for the poor and the needy.

In 1995 Mohammed saw a Muslim Aid video showing scenes of suffering in Bosnia and other war-torn countries. He realised that other people who saw the video would be similarly moved and might donate. In his spare time, he knocked on doors and introduced people to Muslim Aid's work. Crisis in Kosova replaced war in Bosnia, but

Mohammed marches on: neither extreme cold weather nor failing health have stopped him collecting money for the poor and the needy.

Four years on, he has visited nearly every house in High Wycombe and surrounding areas. 'In general, people's responses have been very good. Once they understand who I am, they are happy to donate,' he told *In Focus*, Muslim Aid's annual newsletter. Criticism doesn't bother him. 'If people don't believe I'm from a charity, I just smile and go on to the next house. For each person that does not give there is always one with a big heart who will.'

Mohammed Ashraf is now a well-known figure in High

Wycombe. He visits many people on a monthly basis to keep them informed of Muslim Aid's work and to collect donations. A visit that he will always remember was to a woman who was so moved by the video that she broke down in tears. Despite being very poor herself, she at once donated £100. During another visit, he fell and hurt himself badly. He remembers thinking he was going to die but his belief in what he was doing was stronger. 'Muslim Aid has given me new energy and made me forget my own ill-health.'

Mohammed Ashraf's advice to future volunteers: 'To do this type of work you must keep it very close to your heart.'

1 Explain the difference between disaster relief and development work.
2 Give two examples of each from the information on these two pages.
3 Donors to Muslim Aid can choose to sponsor a specific project. Which of the projects on this page would you choose to sponsor? Explain your choice.

FOCUS TASK

You are working in the publicity department at Muslim Aid. Use the information on pages 98–101 to produce a leaflet or a page for a website to encourage people to give to Muslim Aid. It should include:

- an outline of the origin, aims and aspects of work of Muslim Aid – think about what people might want to know
- a reminder of why it is important for Muslims to care for the poor and needy (supported by quotations from the Qur'an or Hadith)
- ways in which Muslims might help.

Orphan welfare

In 1998 Muslim Aid spent £250,000 on orphan care programmes in ten countries. For example, it supplied much-needed warm winter clothing to 200 Palestinian orphans living in Hebron. In India, Muslim Aid is supporting an orphanage in Tirunelveli, which as well as providing food, shelter and clothing for 250 orphans, also gives them an education and training in skills such as plumbing and radio/TV repair.

Primary healthcare

In 1998, Muslim Aid spent £250,000 on healthcare projects. For example, in Lebanon it provided money for equipment and medicines for a health centre serving the needs of 70,000 people at Ein Elhelwa, the country's largest Palestinian refugee camp. Muslim Aid also funded the building of an emergency accident unit at another Lebanese health centre and provided beds for patients.

Case study: Islam and the National Lottery

As well as giving, Muslims have many other regulations about the use of money, which has led to a whole system of Islamic banking and finance. For example, Islam forbids the earning or charging of interest on loans. In Britain, ordinary banks are increasingly catering for the needs of their many Muslim clients by arranging for any interest earned on their accounts to be channelled directly to their chosen charities. However, other issues are more difficult to resolve.

Like other religious believers, Muslims sometimes find their religious values at odds with secular values. Some say that this is what makes religion interesting, vibrant and dynamic: working out and applying your faith in the real world with real dilemmas. Others worry that important religious principles are compromised by life in the modern world. Which view do you take? Work through the article and questions below and then see if you agree or disagree with the comment in Source G, which was made by one of the advisers on this book.

G

We are all growing up. We are trying our best as Muslims to get to know what Allah wants us to do. And as we grow there are younger ones who will learn from us. Living in a non-Muslim society is a challenge - it is a wonderful opportunity for us to continue to learn.

Akram Khan Cheema

H

REAL WINNERS

Oscar Wilde said he could 'resist everything in life except temptation.' Well he would have jostled to the head of any queue to buy a ticket to win the 'tempting' £18 million National Lottery jackpot. Such was the lottery fever prior to Saturday 10 December 1994 that an estimated 61 million tickets were sold in a week. By now I think you all know who scooped up the mind-boggling millions. But in case you have been meditating in the mountains, here are some clues courtesy of the national newspapers:

'What a happy chap-ati, this Asian immigrant'

'He has curried away the vindaloot'

'Indian father of three is thought to be responsible for the great National Lottery takeaway'

Perhaps the courts should have said something about the racist overtones of the tabloid press. You get the impression that they are piqued that a foreigner should have won so much

money in a lottery clearly designed to keep white working classes in a perpetual stupor. If Karl Marx was alive today he would surely identify the National Lottery as one of the drugs which sedates the people into ignoring the ever-increasing social rot.

The winner must feel wretched, for there is another dimension to this particular chap: he is Muslim and the tabloids have been quick to pick this up. The *Daily Mirror* blasted on its front page '£18 million win's a sin', then devoted a whole page to how the Qur'an

1 **According to Source H:**
a) why is the National Lottery like a drug?
b) why are lottery winnings 'tainted'?
c) how should a Muslim use money won on the lottery?
2 **How and why were the tabloid press racist in their treatment of this story?**
3 **Muslims, like everyone, are tempted to do wrong. But the writer of this article says that the life of a Muslim has to be different.**
a) Why?
b) How might the advice to 'live in this world as though you were a traveller' help Muslims in practice?

ACTIVITY

The author of the *Trends* article says that the lottery winner still has a chance to be 'a real winner on the Day it matters'. Write two stories, one with a positive ending and one with a negative ending, showing what the winner might do with the £18 million.

FOCUS TASK

How can we fund our community centre?
The National Lottery is not an issue that Muslims in Britain today can ignore. The Government is allowing the National Lottery to take over the funding of many projects that would previously have been funded from central or local government budgets. Hospitals, schools, libraries, theatres, sports clubs, community centres, etc., are increasingly dependent on lottery funding. So how does the Muslim approach this issue? The following dilemma was faced by some Yorkshire Muslims in 1998.

In a group, imagine you are a committee drawing up plans for a new community centre in your town. The community centre will cost many hundreds of thousands of pounds. Some money will be raised from the local community, but the only available source of a large grant is the National Lottery. Should they or should they not apply for such funding? In real life the community was divided on this tricky question.

Draw up a list of issues you will need to consider and a process for deciding.

In your group, discuss how Muslims might deal with the issue of using lottery-funded facilities.

declares gamblers as long-term losers. Neither the *Mirror*, nor any of the other tabloids, really know much about Islam. Nevertheless they have played the Muslim-bashing card again. No such indignation when the Prime Minister bought his lottery ticket, despite the strong Jewish–Christian condemnation of gambling.

The Islamic position on the Lottery is quite clear. According to Dr Jamal Badawi, one of the leading Muslim scholars in the western world, 'Lottery is a form of gambling which is prohibited by the Qur'an. It is in the same category as intoxicants.' The personal and social evils of alcohol, drugs and gambling are well known to everyone; so much misery and devastation is caused by their use. Dr Badawi goes on to point out that the wrongdoing (haram) is in the purchasing of the ticket. Therefore every Muslim who buys a ticket commits an unlawful act, irrespective of whether he wins nothing, £10, £1 million or £50 million.

However, as far as the winning is concerned, there are different issues. There is no actual punishment for winning (though the Muslim in Blackburn would disagree, what with all the psychological pressures and family feuds already amok!), but the money is tainted; like the fruits of a forbidden tree. According to Dr Badawi, the £18 million winner (and indeed anyone who has bought a ticket) should first of all seek forgiveness from Allah, remembering that He is all-Merciful, all-Forgiving. Secondly, he should not benefit directly or indirectly from the money. His only option is to use it all for the relief of poverty, destitution or homelessness, etc. He cannot use it for the building of mosques or other religious institutions devoted to the worship of Allah as 'Allah is pure and he loves that which is pure' (Hadith).

Our foolish Muslim from Blackburn finds himself under so much burden. £18 million is a lot to get rid of! But Counsel's Opinion is that the man should not despair. Rather he should take up the challenge of putting the money to its proper use. That is the greatest test for him. If he manages it he will be a winner, a real winner on the Day it matters. By all accounts he is an extremely personable chap: an ideal neighbour and work-mate, sharing his food and helping those in need, working diligently to support his family and give his children a good upbringing and education. Now, by seeking God's forgiveness, he can absolve himself of his £1 folly. That is not the problem, as Allah says, 'I am truly forgiving' (Surah 15.49). His test lies in giving away £18 million.

Like Oscar Wilde, our Muslim could not resist the temptation. Indeed, most people in the UK couldn't. But the life of a Muslim is different, it has to be. Did not the blessed Prophet say 'Live in this world as though you were a traveller'?

Trends, December 1994. In this feature called 'Counsel's Opinion' leading Islamic scholars comment on contemporary issues.

5.2 Live in this world as if you were going to live forever!

A

B

C

ACTIVITY

Look at Sources A, B and C. Make up a short story about one of these photographs. Think about:

a) what is happening
b) what human actions, deliberate or accidental, might have contributed to this environmental problem
c) what human actions or other circumstances might solve this problem.

Think creatively. There are no right answers to this question.

Masters or servants of Allah's creation?

Muslims believe that Allah created the universe and all life on Earth (see pages 30–31). They see the environment as Allah's creation to be treated with respect. 'Creation' means the same thing to a Muslim as 'environment' might to a non-Muslim.

Islam teaches that Allah made the Earth a good place with everything that is needed for a good life for humans and all other living creatures. Allah gave all human beings responsibility to care for it.

Creation does not *belong* to human beings. It belongs to Allah. People have the role of Khalifah. They are 'stewards' or 'guardians' of creation – they look after something which is not theirs. Human beings must guard the creation for Allah. At the Day of Judgement Muslims will be called to account for how well they have done this.

Within Allah's creation life is finely balanced. To waste its resources or harm parts of it would be to disobey Allah. So, for example:

- Muslims must make careful use of scarce resources such as water
- hunting is allowed only for food, not for pleasure
- a tree should be planted where possible whenever one is cut down.

FOCUS TASK

Each of these green jigsaw pieces contains an Islamic teaching that helps to show Muslims how and why they should care for the environment.

1 It is He who has made you His agents …
So He may test you in the way you use the gifts He has given you.

Surah 6.165

2 If anyone plants a tree or sows a field and men, beasts or birds eat from it, he should consider it as a charity on his part.

Hadith: Imam Ahmad, Musnad Volume IV

3 Live in this world as if you were going to live forever …

Bukhari Hadith

4 O children of Adam! … eat and drink: but do not waste by being greedy, for Allah does not love wasters.

Surah 7.31

5 There is not an animal that lives on Earth, nor a being that flies on its wings, which isn't living in communities like you.

Surah 6.38

6 How can you reject the faith in Allah? …
It is He who has created all things on Earth for you.

Surah 2.28–9

7 Consider the water which you drink.
Was it you that brought it down … or did We?
If it was Our Will, We could make it salty.
Why then do you not give thanks?

Surah 56.68–70

8 Do Allah's work according to the pattern He set out for mankind:
Let there be no change in the work planned by Allah.

Surah 30.30

Each of these blue pieces shows an instruction.

1 **Match each instruction piece to one of the teachings. Your teacher can give you worksheets of all the pieces.**
2 **Use the rest of this investigation and your own knowledge to give one example of an application of each instruction.**

a) Look after Allah's creation

b) Use creation for the good of others

c) Don't waste resources

d) Keep to Allah's plan

e) Communal living is part of Allah's plan

f) Let creation point you to Allah

g) Think long term

h) Be grateful

instruction — quotation — example

Case study: Fazlun Khalid

Fazlun Khalid is Founder Director of the Islamic Foundation for Ecology and Environmental Sciences (IFEES).

Fazlun was born in Sri Lanka and came to Britain in 1953. He served in the RAF for ten years, then worked for the Commission for Racial Equality.

Two issues led to his concern for the environment.

The first was poverty. Sri Lanka was a British colony for many years. It was run for the benefit of Britain and not for the benefit of the Sri Lankan people. Despite all the wealth generated under the colonial government, most Sri Lankans remained very poor. This worried Fazlun.

The second was his work with immigrant communities in Britain. He found that stable families were often broken down by the experience of immigration. They came to unnatural concrete jungles that were depressing places to live. It seemed to Fazlun that this was one cause of the breakdown of community. Through the 1970s and 1980s he worked with others to help Muslim families to rebuild a sense of community in Leeds and Birmingham. He believed that people needed to reconnect with the environment for their own good and for the good of creation. The quotations on these two pages are from our interview with him.

1 Compare the title of this investigation (5.2) with the last words of the previous one (5.1), see page 103. How can you explain these different pieces of advice?

A few hundred years ago, when most people lived close to the land, people lived with an instinct for the natural order. They lived as if they were part of creation, not masters of it. For Muslims, this is the idea of living within the balance of the created order. People understood the cycle of seasons and the cycle of life because they were surrounded by the natural world. Of course, some people polluted rivers and cut down forests in those days, but they lived within the limits of the natural order. There were limits to their own power.

With new beliefs and changes in society the balance has changed. There's a change in perception from being part of God's creation to being masters of it. The meaning of Islam is submission. Islam is totally opposed to the secular idea of the lordship of human beings. Islam teaches submission to Allah and to Allah's created order.

There's also this belief in endless growth, which is fired by borrowing and credit. The banking system makes money out of nothing. It then seeks people to lend it to. The financial system demands growth, growth, growth. But the world cannot sustain endless growth.

Now the Earth's resources are being destroyed – for ever. Despite the teachings of the Qur'an, Muslims have done little about the situation in the past. They have left it to governments and international agencies. But we believe that the time has come to safeguard our future in this world. We have to apply the Qur'an and Sunnah to modern environmental issues. We have to take positive action. Allah entrusted man with the guardianship of the Earth; we have to fulfil that ancient trust now – before it is too late.

Read page 107.
2 How can the work of IFEES help Muslims to apply their faith to environmental issues?
3 a) What problems do you think IFEES might face in setting up their model community?
b) How could those problems be overcome?

DISCUSS

1 What are Fazlun Khalid's criticisms of the banking system?
2 What do you think he means by this?
3 Why is Islam against charging interest on loans? (see page 102)
4 What are the consequences of borrowing more money than you can pay back:
  a) for the individual
  b) for a country?

Level 1: the individual

Individuals can make a great difference to the quality of the environment. Your lifestyle, the goods that you buy, the way you act all play their part in helping or harming the environment. Recently the British government pointed out that if every person in Britain turned off their electronic equipment at night, instead of leaving it on stand-by, enough electricity would be saved to close one (acid-rain-producing) power station.

What are the responsibilities of the individual Muslim?

1. Seek understanding

This is most important. What was once an instinctive understanding of the natural world now has to be learned. People have to be educated. If you live in a concrete urban jungle where there are few trees and no natural features you need to learn about the natural world. So Muslims should educate themselves and educate others about the fragility of the natural world and human dependence on it.

2. Consume less

It's the same for Muslims as for all citizens. Reduce what you buy, reduce what you use, little by little. This is hard, since all the pressures of modern life drive in the opposite direction.

- If you have two cars, cut down to one.
- If you have one car, think twice before you use it. Cycle or use public transport instead.
- Use less water. When you wash for prayer – use less water.

Level 2: working together

The individual can achieve a lot, but collective action is stronger still. IFEES brings Muslims together to build links with other environmental agencies, for example the World Wide Fund for Nature and major Islamic relief agencies such as Muslim Aid (see pages 100–101).

> One of our big hopes for the future is to build a model Islamic land-based community in a rural setting in England. Muslims with various skills can apply the Qur'an and Sunnah to environmental issues, working on:
>
> - research and resources
> - training for all age groups, based on the Qur'an
> - organic farming
> - intermediate technology (such as solar energy).
>
> It would set an example to others and provide a source of information and advice.

Villagers work together securing sand dunes to fight desertification in the Sahara in Mauritania.

- Use less fossil fuel – gas, petrol, coal.
- Grow your own vegetables.
- At the supermarket, buy the goods with less elaborate packaging.
- Recycle paper. Use recycled paper.

3. Work with others

Muslims are not in this alone, which leads to level 2 . . .

E

An Arabian oryx

I There are many hadith where Muhammad ﷺ calls on Muslims to care for animals. But sometimes in the real world there are difficult choices to make.

In pairs, list acceptable and unacceptable uses of animals and discuss your lists as a class. You can get a sheet from your teacher to help you explore this issue.

Level 3: government action

Muslims are expected to show respect for all parts of Allah's creation. This also applies to governments who claim to follow Islamic principles.

Oman: an Islamic environmental policy

The Sultan of Oman was inspired by his faith to adopt new Islamic environmental policies in his country. The first laws concerning the environment were passed in 1974, hunting for sport was banned in 1975 and a Ministry of the Environment was set up in 1984.

In Oman, as in neighbouring Saudi Arabia and other countries of the Arabian Peninsula, there are traditional areas of protected, undeveloped land called HEMA. Muhammad ﷺ said that 'hema is only for Allah and His Prophet', and so, even if such land is owned by an individual or the government, it should be treated as belonging to the community and should only be used for the common good.

Under the new environmental policies, these areas are protected by law, and local communities are involved in conservation management (see case study below).

A coastal zone management project has carried out a detailed ecological survey. As a result, Oman is now one of the world's most closely studied environments for management purposes. This knowledge can benefit environmentalists in other countries. Other projects have focused more on preserving Oman's diverse natural beauty.

With this commitment to the environment backed by faith, it was natural for the Sultan of Oman to adopt the Assisi Declaration of 1986 (see opposite).

Case study: 'Operation Oryx'

In 1960 concern was first raised by environmental groups about the situation of the Arabian oryx. Hunting in the Arabian Peninsula meant there were only 100–200 oryx left living wild, in one remote part of the Arabian desert. Continued hunting threatened their complete extinction so Operation Oryx was launched by a number of voluntary agencies.

Three of the last remaining wild oryx were caught. Careful breeding of zoo oryx began.

In 1972 the Arabian oryx was declared extinct in the wild: there were no wild oryx left. However, the zoo population, or 'world herd', as they became known, was increasing.

In 1976 the Sultan of Oman began actively supporting the work and in 1982 ten of the herd were released into the wild in Oman, under the protection of a local community. For example, the habitat of the Arabian oryx is guarded by members of the local Harasis tribe, acting as rangers. The Harasis people now regard the oryx as their tribal property and, under their protection, numbers have increased.

These animals were carefully monitored and the first truly 'wild' calves were born soon after. A second herd was released in Oman in 1983. Saudi Arabia followed some years later by introducing its own herds to the wild.

In Oman, other species such as the houbara bustard, a desert bird also hunted almost to extinction, have also benefited from this scheme and other similar ones.

SAVE AS ...

Write a 150-word press release for an Islamic news agency celebrating the birth of the first wild calves to the oryx released in 1982. Make sure the press release mentions Islamic beliefs about the project.

Give your press release a headline.

F

Behold! In the creation of the heavens and the Earth,
And in the alternation of night and day –
There are indeed Signs for men of understanding –
Men who celebrate the praises of Allah, standing, sitting and lying down.

Surah 3.190–91

Hindu, Buddhist, Christian and Muslim representatives at the Assisi Declaration

2 Why do you think this event was called a pilgrimage?
3 How effective do you think the Assisi and Ohito Declarations might be? Explain your answer.

G

Allah's trustees are responsible for maintaining the unity of His creation, its flora, its fauna, its wildlife and natural environment … Unity cannot be had by setting one need against another or one end over another; it is maintained by balance and harmony.

From the Muslim declaration on 'religion and nature'

Level 4: international action

Many modern environmental issues are now so wide-ranging and complex that they need an international response. Can religion help?

The Assisi Declaration

In 1986 Muslims were among representatives of all the main world religions on an international pilgrimage to Assisi. The event marked the twenty-fifth anniversary of the World Wide Fund for Nature. Assisi was the home of the Christian St Francis (1181–1226) who had emphasised a need to be at one with God's creation.

From all over the world, all the pilgrims met up in the old Basilica (church) of St Francis. There, during a multi-faith service, they gave thanks for the world and all that is in it and, as people of faith, declared their responsibility for it and the role they would play in protecting it. The call to prayer was made by a muezzin in the words of Surah 3.190–91 (Source F).

At the conference representatives of each religion made their own declaration of the part they would play in conserving nature. Source F contains extracts from the Muslim declaration.

The Ohito Declaration

The Assisi Declaration was followed nine years later by the Ohito Declaration on Religions, Land and Conservation which published guidelines for future action. Fazlun Khalid (see pages 106–107) is responsible for coordinating work under the Ohito Declaration in the UK.

FOCUS TASK

Action on the environment could be compared to ripples on a pond spreading outwards from a centre.

1   **Cut out five different-sized circles. The smallest one should be at least 8 cm in diameter.**
2   **Starting with the smallest, label these circles around their outside edge: Islamic teaching on Allah's creation, individual action, collective action, government action, international action.**
3   **Using what you have learned from pages 104–109, write statements to guide people working at each level on how to help Muslims preserve and celebrate Allah's creation. Give one example of action at each level.**
4   **Pin your circles together like this to make a ripple diagram.**

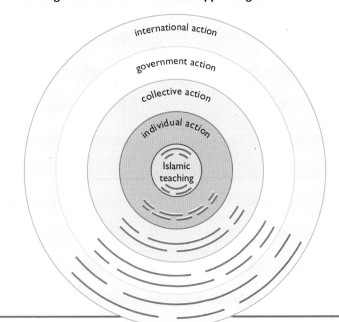

5.3 Is it ever right to fight?

One meaning of the word 'Islam' is 'peace'. When two Muslims meet, the first words they usually say to each other are:

As-Salamu alaykum (Peace be with you)

Wa alaykum Salam (And also with you)

Most people in the world want peace for themselves and for others, but despite this, most would also agree that it is hard to achieve.

The big religious question is, why is peace so hard to achieve when most people want it? Some people say that the problem lies in human nature itself. The following stories from the beginnings of Islam show how Muhammad ﷺ tried to deal with the problems of peace and war.

Peace-making in Madinah

File Edit Insert Format Tools Table Window **?**

Makkah 620CE
Life has become difficult for Muhammad ﷺ and his fellow Muslims. Since beginning to preach Allah's message, he has made many enemies in Makkah.

The new leader of Muhammad's ﷺ clan is a bitter opponent of Muhammad ﷺ. The clan wants to stop him preaching his message of one God. They fear he will damage their trade, which depends on idol-worshipping pilgrims coming to the Kab'ah. Muhammad's ﷺ life has been threatened.

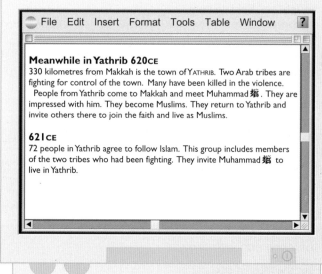

File Edit Insert Format Tools Table Window **?**

Meanwhile in Yathrib 620CE
330 kilometres from Makkah is the town of YATHRIB. Two Arab tribes are fighting for control of the town. Many have been killed in the violence.

People from Yathrib come to Makkah and meet Muhammad ﷺ. They are impressed with him. They become Muslims. They return to Yathrib and invite others there to join the faith and live as Muslims.

621CE
72 people in Yathrib agree to follow Islam. This group includes members of the two tribes who had been fighting. They invite Muhammad ﷺ to live in Yathrib.

FOCUS TASK

1 **An important aim of Source A was to help establish Madinah as one ummah – a community of believers living harmoniously instead of as separate warring tribes. Here are six principles designed to achieve this. Match each principle to one or more points of the 'Constitution':**

- **all costs must be shared**
- **all believers are equal, whatever their religion**
- **people have the right to their own religion**
- **Allah is the ruler of the ummah**
- **people must try to settle problems peacefully instead of by fighting**
- **the ummah will fight together to defend itself from outsiders**

A

1. The Jews and the Muslims from Makkah and Madinah are all one ummah.
2. Any Jew who follows us has the same rights as anyone else in the ummah.
3. No believer is allowed to protect a member of the Quraysh or his wealth.
4. Any Jew who is with the believers shall share the expenses of the believers.
5. The Jews and the Muslims each have their own religion.
6. The Jews and the Muslims will help one another, consult one another and not fight one another.
7. Madinah is a place of sanctuary for the ummah.
8. Any disagreement which cannot be settled shall be referred to Allah and Allah's messenger, Muhammad.
9. All members of the ummah shall join together and defend Madinah in case of attack.
10. Anyone who is told to stop fighting must do so in the interests of peace.

2 **Look at the list that you made in answer to the Activity on page 110. Choose three items on your list and explain whether or not the measures in Source A might help control these aspects of human nature.**

3 **Five years after the agreement in Source A all the Jews in Madinah had either become Muslims or left the town. Does this affect your view of this agreement?**

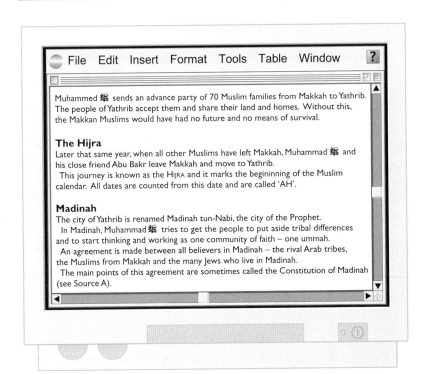

File   Edit   Insert   Format   Tools   Table   Window   ?

Muhammed 🕌 sends an advance party of 70 Muslim families from Makkah to Yathrib. The people of Yathrib accept them and share their land and homes. Without this, the Makkan Muslims would have had no future and no means of survival.

The Hijra
Later that same year, when all other Muslims have left Makkah, Muhammad 🕌 and his close friend Abu Bakr leave Makkah and move to Yathrib.
 This journey is known as the HIJRA and it marks the begininning of the Muslim calendar. All dates are counted from this date and are called 'AH'.

Madinah
The city of Yathrib is renamed Madinah tun-Nabi, the city of the Prophet.
 In Madinah, Muhammad 🕌 tries to get the people to put aside tribal differences and to start thinking and working as one community of faith – one ummah.
 An agreement is made between all believers in Madinah – the rival Arab tribes, the Muslims from Makkah and the many Jews who live in Madinah.
 The main points of this agreement are sometimes called the Constitution of Madinah (see Source A).

I In groups discuss:
a) does winning a battle prove that God is on your side?
b) does losing a battle mean that God is against you?

ACTIVITY

In groups of about six people, imagine you are a radio news team in 624CE (2AH). You have:
a) a reporter on the battle front at Badr with the Muslim forces
b) a reporter in Makkah, receiving regular reports from the Makkan army
c) a presenter and several experts in the studio.

The reporter in Makkah has informed the studio that the two armies have just met and that the fighting has begun. You have twenty minutes to prepare a five-minute news bulletin.
    Your live broadcast is interrupted by news from the front of the Muslims victory. Include this.

SAVE AS ...

I Explain why the Battle of Badr took place and describe what happened.
2 What do you think were the effects of their victory on the faith of the Muslims in Madinah? Give reasons.
3 Do you think it was right for the two armies to fight each other? Give reasons for your opinion showing you have thought about different points of view.

Collective defense at Badr: Why was the Battle of Badr necessary?

On page 111 you read about the establishment of the new Muslim community at Madinah. This did not end the enmity between the Muslims and the Quraysh leaders in Makkah. For many years the two parties were in a constant state of conflict. This led to the Battle of Badr in 624CE.

Background

The Makkans virtually forced the Muslims to leave Makkah. Once most of the Muslims had left, the Makkans seized the property they had left behind and continued to attack any relatives who had stayed in Makkah. The Quraysh regarded the Muslims as disloyal because they had made an alliance with two other Arab tribes in Madinah. The Muslims for their part now regarded loyalty to Islam as being more important than tribal loyalty.

Muhammad's plan

Two years after Muhammad had gone to live in Madinah, Abu Sufyan, the Quraysh leader, was returning from Syria with a large caravan (which included goods bought with property stolen from the Muslims). Muhammad led a force of 300 from Madinah to attack the caravan.

The Makkan plan

A 1000-strong army, led by Abu Jahl and other Makkan leaders, was sent from Makkah to defend it. They intended to teach the Muslims a lesson and make Muhammad appear a weak leader, incapable of protecting his people.

Face to face

Muhammad gathered together as many able-bodied men and boys as he could and moved quickly southwards to face the Makkan threat.

Thirsty

After their long march, the Makkan soldiers were desperately in need of water to refresh them and prepare them for battle. But Muhammad had cut off their path to the wells at Badr. This left the Makkans exhausted and unable to fight at full strength.

Praying for victory

Even though Muhammad's army was outnumbered by more than three to one, their opponents were exhausted and the Muslims believed that Allah was on their side. Would this be enough to defeat their enemies? They prayed to Allah for help.

The battle

The Qur'an says that Allah answered their prayers by sending one thousand angels to fight with them. The Muslims were victorious and many of the Makkan leaders were killed or captured.

The results

As a result of their defeat, the Makkans had to recognise that Muhammad was a powerful leader and that the Muslims were a force to be reckoned with. For the Muslims, their victory at Badr confirmed their belief that Allah was on their side and that they had an extraordinary leader.

B

Conditions for 'jihad' or collective defence
Muslims can only be involved in a collective defence when:

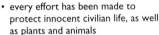

• all other ways of trying to settle a dispute have failed

• every effort has been made to protect innocent civilian life, as well as plants and animals

• they are not being allowed to practise their religion freely

• it has been declared by a religious leader whose authority is accepted by the Muslim community. All able-bodied Muslim men must fight

• the community is suffering under a tyrant; it is under attack and needs to restore its freedom

What does Islam teach about war?

Despite its emphasis on peace-making, Islam is sometimes perceived as a war-like religion. This stereotype is fed not only by the British media who misunderstand many aspects of Muslim life, but also by regimes (that claim to be Islamic) around the world who wage war for supposedly Islamic principles. Some Muslims (like some members of other religions) do wage war and justify that war in religious terms, but all too often that war does not meet the very strict rules proposed by the Qur'an for a *just* (fair) war.

Islam is a practical religion. On occasions during their history Muslims have needed to defend themselves when their rights have been under attack. In the first days of Islam, many Muslims lost their lives trying to defend their beliefs and values. Islam recognises that there will always be conflict between people. So on the one hand the Qur'an provides rules for living which should minimise conflict but on the other it also provides rules for war. For example, Allah teaches in the Qur'an that Muslims should only fight in order to defend Islam; they should never attack other people or try to use violence to convert them to Islam. So how do Muslims decide whether or not war is acceptable to Allah? (Source B.)

What does 'jihad' really mean?

'Jihad' is the word used to describe the personal struggle of each Muslim against evil as they try to follow the way of Allah (see page 18). Sometimes this struggle can involve the Muslim in the collective armed defence of the Muslim community, although physical fighting is not the main meaning of jihad.

In the Battle of Badr Muhammad 🕌 led the Muslims into battle to defend the safety of the Muslims in Madinah. Muslims would say that this battle was a jihad because all those who were able joined in. They were defending themselves against Makkan violence. Their intention was to attack the caravan, not to start a war.

Jihad misunderstood

The word 'jihad' is often misused to describe any war involving Muslims. It is also misused by Muslim political leaders to justify a war they want to wage.

However, all too often these wars do not meet the conditions required for jihad. A war is not jihad if:

1 war is declared by a political leader rather than a religious leader
2 an individual declares war without the support of the Muslim community
3 war is declared in attack, rather than defence
4 war is declared to win new land or power
5 war is declared to try to convert others to Islam
6 peaceful ways of solving the conflict have not been tried
7 innocent civilians, particularly women and children, are exposed to physical danger
8 trees, crops and animals have not been protected.

ACTIVITY A

With a partner, match each of the quotations in Source C
with one condition for jihad in Source B on page 113.

C

1 *Three men refused to go out to battle with
everyone else. They complained they had too
many jobs to do, too many dates to harvest.
Muhammad* 🌼 *responded firmly, refusing to
speak to them and forbidding other Muslims to
have anything to do with them.*

Hadith

2 *Abu Bakr, the first Khalifah [successor to the
Prophet] said, 'Do not be harsh on them; do not kill
children, old men or women; do not cut down or
burn palm trees, do not destroy fruit trees, do not
slay a sheep or camel except for food. If you see
people who have taken refuge in monasteries, let
them be safe in their place of refuge.'*

Islam the natural way by Abdul Wahid Hamid

3 *If two parties among the Believers fall into a
       quarrel,
Make peace between them:
But if one of them goes too far against the other,
Then all of you must fight against the one that goes
       too far
Until they do what is expected of them by Allah.*

Surah 49.9

4 *If people declare war against you, you may fight
       back, because you have been wronged by
       them –
Truly, Allah is Most Powerful for your aid
When you have been turned out of your home,
       which is not right,
The only reason this has happened to you is
       because you have publicly stated your belief
       in Allah.*

Surah 22.39–40

5 *The Prophet said,
'Help your brother, whether he is the oppressor or
the oppressed.' When they asked him how they
could help one who was an oppressor, he said,
'Restrain him from it.'*

Hadith

6 *And hold fast,
All together, by the Rope
Which Allah stretches out
For you, and be not divided
Among yourselves.*

Surah 3.103

ACTIVITY B

You now know quite a lot about Muslim attitudes to peace
and to war. You can see that the conditions for jihad are
very strict. Even so, there are examples today where
many Muslims would believe an armed struggle could fulfil
all the conditions for jihad established by the Qur'an and
Sunnah. You are going to use your knowledge of Islamic
teaching in the following role play.

In groups of five to eight people, imagine you are
Muslims living in a remote village. Whenever there is a
problem that affects the whole village you all gather
together to decide what is to be done.

Four people come to address your meeting. Each has a
story to tell. Each is hoping for your help (see opposite).

Decide how your meeting is usually organised and
consider each story separately.

Your small village has limited resources. You will only
be able to support one of the people; you may decide that
you are unable to help any of them.

You must come to a decision on which you all agree.

SAVE AS ...

For the case you chose to support (or another one if you
prefer) write a description of 'what happened next'.
You could write it as a story in the first person as if you
were one of the people who helped, or you could write as
a neutral observer. However you write, make sure you
show how Islamic values play a part in the events.

As well as referring to this investigation, you can also
bring in ideas from earlier in this book. For example, you
might want to refer to the individual in society (pages
18–22), evil and suffering (pages 40–45), the ummah
(pages 66–71) and racism (pages 89–95).

1   I need your help. Last night my house was attacked. I was in a field tending to my goats when raiders kicked in the door. They have stolen the few valuable possessions we had and smashed up our furniture. One of them tried to molest my daughter! What would have happened if I had not disturbed them?

It was Ali's men – I saw them. That man is a murdering thief. Help me to sort him out, give him a taste of his own medicine! It could be one of your homes or one of your daughters he goes for next!

2   I need your help. I have come from the capital to warn you that our country is facing an invasion from foreign troops. A build-up of tanks and armoured vehicles has been seen on the borders in the south. We have heard that they are heavily armed. It seems that they want to use our country to shield them from their enemies in the north.

Our country is in great danger. You probably feel that you are safe from attack up here in the hills, that no one will bother you. Maybe you are right; but I beg you to think of your fellow citizens down on the plains. They will surely lose their freedom, even their lives, if you do not come to their help!

3   I need your help. For too long now the villagers in these hills have been at the mercy of our rulers in the capital. They expect us to run to their help at the first sign of trouble from outside, but what do they do for us? When did we last see any foreign aid? Who looks after us when floods destroy our houses or drought kills our crops?

It is time for us to take our destiny into our own hands. We must gather together all the able-bodied adults from all the hill-villages. March to the capital! Demand more aid! More money! We must fight, with force if necessary, for our rights. We must not give in to them any more!

4   I need your help. I am from the next village. A group of religious extremists have come to my village and set up a base. They seem to be rich and they are tempting the young people with offers of a new life in another country if they reject Islam and convert to their religion.

One or two have already rebelled against their parents and gone with these missionaries. We have tried to reason with them, but it is as if they have been brainwashed! What can we do? We are so poor and these people claim to offer riches beyond our wildest dreams.

You are fellow Muslims! Help us to protect our faith and these vulnerable young people! Let's drive away these meddlesome unbelievers!

Peace-making in Palestine: the Open House project

Ramle is a small town between Tel Aviv and Jerusalem in Israel. The population of 55,000 consists of about 18 per cent Arabs and 82 per cent Jews – about the same proportions as in Israel as a whole.

But Ramle is not typical of this country in one very important respect. Here a community of Muslims, Jews and Christians are living together in a spirit of reconciliation and peace.

In the 1948 war, shortly after the founding of the state of Israel, almost all the Arab residents of Ramle were forced to leave their homes. One of these families was the Al-Khayris, who were Muslims.

In 1967, after the Six-Day War, the Al-Khayris returned to Ramle and for the first time met Dalia Landau, a Jewish woman who had grown up in the same house the Al-Khayris had called home all those years before. They became friends at once and twenty-four years later, in April 1991, they decided to dedicate their house to the children of Ramle. A Palestinian Christian who was a city councillor was made the project's director.

Their project was called Open House. The project has two main purposes:

- to provide educational and social opportunities for Arab children and their families
- to be a centre where Jews and Palestinians can meet one another, enjoy group activities and make friends.

The activities at Open House include:

- nursery education facilities (very few are available in Israel for Arab children)
- summer camps for Jewish and Palestinian teenagers
- a centre for Jewish–Arab co-existence.

Global issues – Review tasks

A

Look at Source A.

1 Explain the meaning of the term 'zakah'.

2 Write a paragraph to describe the aims and the work of Muslim Aid.

3 Choose and explain two pieces of teaching from the Qur'an or the Hadith that might influence a Muslim to support Muslim Aid.

4 'Muslim Aid should merge with aid agencies of other religions.' Do you agree?
Explain your answer showing that you have considered other points of view.

B

1 Explain the meaning of the term 'Khalifah'.

2 State and explain one quotation from the Qur'an that could encourage a Muslim to be a good Khalifah.

3 How might this teaching affect a Muslim's response to the plight of the refugees described in Source A?

C

1 Explain the meaning of the term 'jihad'.

2 Write a paragraph to explain the conditions for 'collective defense'.

3 'A war that causes suffering to civilians cannot be a just war.' Do you agree? Explain your answer showing that you have considered other points of view.

A

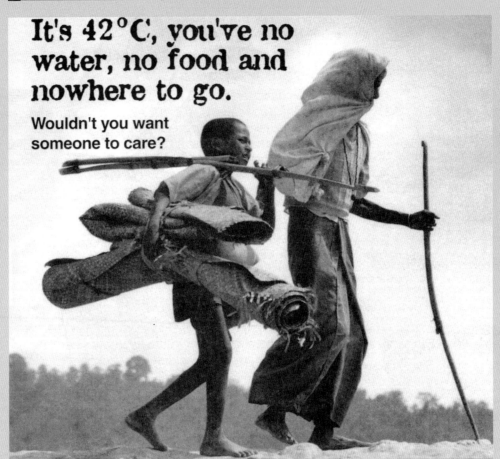

It's 42°C, you've no water, no food and nowhere to go.

Wouldn't you want someone to care?

These are typical of the conditions that face millions of refugees in many parts of the world. Every day is a struggle to survive.

Since its inception in 1985, Muslim Aid has helped millions of refugees around the world by providing emergency relief and initiating rehabilitation projects.

But the suffering, however, seems endless. There is always much more needed to be done. Your donation to Muslim Aid can help ensure that urgent support could be provided to those in need.

Muslim Aid

Dept. FA52,
P. O. Box 3,
London N7 8LR.

Yes! I would like to help refugees. I enclose cheque/postal order for £_____ (Zakah/General)

Mr/Mrs/Miss _____ Address _____

_____

Postcode _____ Telephone ( ) _____

A handbill for Muslim Aid

Conclusion

You've reached the end of your course. How will it be useful to you?

Your exam

Your chief concern is probably to get a good grade in your exam. We have helped you in various ways. Here is a reminder of the ideas you will need to bear in mind when you revise for your exam.

Different traditions

Muslims have a range of views. In your exam, you will need to show that you understand how and why different Muslims have different attitudes to moral and theological issues.

You will improve your grade if you can show your grasp of the differences between Muslim traditions, or between Islam and another religion, on moral issues.

Sources of authority

You have examined the ways Muslims use sources such as the Qur'an and Hadith or their religious leaders as authorities.

You will improve your grade if you can not only name the sources of authority used by Muslims, but also show how they use each source of authority.

Absolute and relative

You have investigated the difference between an absolute approach to morality and a relative approach and have recorded your own examples of absolute and relative responses to different issues.

You will improve your grade if you can refer to absolute and relative morality confidently. You should show you understand that they are not watertight definitions; rather, they show an 'approach' to decision-making on certain issues by certain traditions.

Core beliefs

You have studied some of the core beliefs that lie at the heart of Muslim thinking on moral issues.

You will improve your grade if you can not only describe such beliefs, but also demonstrate how these beliefs inspire Muslims and affect their values and their actions. Islam is a living faith, evolving year by year as its followers meet new challenges. This course is about real-life Islam. It is your understanding of the relationship between these beliefs and Muslim values and actions that will interest the examiner.

Your own views

This course has given you plenty of opportunity to express your own views and to give reasons for them. You may be surprised that even this will be useful in your exam.

Sometimes you are specifically asked for your view in an exam question. The reasons for your opinion, and your ability to back it up, interest the examiner more than the viewpoint itself. So, remember: you will improve your grade if you can express your own views on issues you have tackled, and explain and support them with reference to the Muslim ideas you have studied in this book.

Your beliefs and values

One of the aims of Religious Education is to learn from religion. Religion gives its followers beliefs and values to live by. This course has encouraged you to debate, to understand and to make your own decisions about Muslims' beliefs and values. The beliefs and values you have studied in this course may be similar to your own or they may be different. In either case, this course should have helped you to clarify your own beliefs and values.

RE-EVALUATION

At the beginning of this book you recorded your own views on the relevance of studying Islam. Has your view changed at all? If so, how and why?

FOCUS TASK

The illustration shows some values that Muslims might think were important to help guide people in their moral decision-making.

1 **Choose three that you would like to take with you into the future. Explain your choice.**
2 **Explain whether you reject any of the values altogether and, if so, why.**
3 **For your three chosen values, give an example of how they might affect your actions in the future.**

Glossary

abortion (1) the termination of a pregnancy before the fetus is sufficiently developed to survive (2) operation to cause this

absolute morality belief that there is a right course of action in a moral dilemma that is true in all situations

Abu Bakr Muhammad's ﷺ father-in-law and friend and first Khalifah

adhan the call to salah

Al-Mahdi 'the Rightly Guided one who is awaited' – Shi'ah Muslims believe the twelfth Imam will return again as Al-Mahdi (the Messiah)

Al-Fatihah 'The Opening' – name of the first surah of the Qur'an

Ali Muhammad's ﷺ cousin and son-in-law and fourth Khalifah; Shi'ah Muslims also believe he was the first of 12 Imams

Allah Arabic word for God

capital punishment killing someone as punishment

da'wah inviting people to Islam

Dhikr 'remembrance' – the names of Allah or short phrases from the Qur'an are recited over and over again

discrimination the action of treating someone unfairly because of a prejudice

du'a 'calling upon' – personal prayers

euthanasia ending a person's life deliberately but for compassionate reasons to end suffering:
(1) active – something is done to a person, e.g. they are given drugs, to make them die more quickly
(2) compulsory/involuntary – someone else, e.g. a doctor or family member, decides it would be in the person's best interests to end their life
(3) passive – any form of treatment which might extend a person's life is taken away, e.g. a life support machine is turned off
(4) voluntary – a person asks for their life to be ended

fard actions that have to be done – category of halal

Fatimah Al-Zahrah Ali's wife and Muhammad's ﷺ youngest daughter

fatwa legal guidance made by knowledgeable Muslims based on the Qur'an, Sunnah and Shari'ah

fitrah spirituality and instinctive need of Allah which makes everyone capable of recognising the presence of Allah; also gives people an instinctive moral sense

general revelation indirect revelation about Allah available to everyone; some truths about Allah can be revealed through the natural world, through reason, through conscience or through moral sense

hadith/Hadith stories about or sayings of Muhammad ﷺ

Hafiz title given to Muslims who learn the entire Qur'an by heart

Hajj annual pilgrimage to Makkah that every Muslim must complete at least once in their life if he or she is healthy and can afford it

halal 'behaviour which is permitted'

haram 'behaviour which is forbidden'

hema traditional areas of protected, undeveloped land which should be treated as belonging to the community and only used for the common good

hijab veiled clothing

Hijra journey Muhammad ﷺ made from Makkah to Yathrib in 622CE; marks the beginning of the Muslim calendar

human-made suffering suffering caused by human actions

ibadah 'worship' – the main acts of ibadah are the five pillars of Islam

Ibrahim (Abraham) one of the five main prophets of Islam

iddah waiting period, usually of three months, to allow time for reflection and reconciliation after a pronouncement of divorce

Id-ul-Fitr festival that marks the end of the fast during the month of Ramadan

ihram the state entered into to perform Hajj

ihsan 'perfection'

imam leader; in Sunni Islam the imam leads communal prayer; in Shi'ah Islam 'Imam' is the title of Ali and his successors

iman 'faith' or 'belief'

immanent 'present in the universe' – used to describe Allah as part of human life, able to act in human affairs and affect daily life

Isa (Jesus) one of the five main prophets of Islam

Jibril (Gabriel) an angel

jihad every Muslim's individual struggle to resist evil in order to follow the path of Allah; also 'collective defence'

jinn unseen beings, created by Allah, who have free will

jumu'ah weekly communal prayers performed shortly after midday on Fridays

Ka'bah cube-shaped building in the centre of the Grand Mosque in Makkah, most holy Muslim shrine

Khadijah Muhammad's ﷺ first wife

Khalifah 'successor', 'vicegerent', 'inheritor'

'khul a woman who wants to end her marriage can arrange for compensation for her husband

khutbah speech delivered by imam, e.g. during prayers in a mosque

liberation theology belief that religious believers should be involved in political action on the side of the poor

Madinah Madinah tun-Nabi (The City of the Prophet). The new name given to Yathrib after Muhammad ﷺ journeyed there from Makkah in 622CE (the Hijra)

mahr marriage gift that the groom must give to his bride

mahrib niche or alcove in the wall of a mosque indicating the qiblah

Makkah birthplace of Muhammad ﷺ, site of the Ka'bah, and most holy city of Islam

makruh actions that are disapproved of although not forbidden – category of halal

mandub actions that are recommended – category of halal

marj'ah representative of the Imam; followed by Shi'ah Muslims in the absence of the Imam (*plural*: marj'anah)

masjid Arabic word for 'mosque', literally 'place of prostration'

minbar raised platform from which the imam delivers the khutbah

monotheist believer in one God; Islam is a monotheistic religion

mubah actions that may be done – category of halal

muezzin ('mu'adhdhin' in Arabic) – someone who calls Muslims to prayer from a minaret on the mosque

Muhammad ﷺ Allah's last prophet; he received the revelation of the Qur'an from Allah

Musa (Moses) one of the five main prophets of Islam

nafs the selfishness that is within everyone

natural suffering suffering caused by an event beyond human control

nikah the contract of marriage. It means marriage and all the legal issues relating to it

niyyah 'intention' – before all acts of worship Muslims state their intention to please Allah

Nuh (Noah) one of the five main prophets of Islam

polytheist believer in more than one god

prejudice the attitude of having an opinion which is not based on fact

Qadr predestination; belief that everything that happens is part of Allah's plan

qiblah the direction of the Ka'bah in Makkah; Muslims face qiblah when they perform salah

Qur'an Muslim sacred text, meaning 'recitation' – Allah's final revelation to humankind, received and transmitted through Muhammad ﷺ

relative morality belief that different courses of action might be needed in different situations

sacred holy, set apart for God

sadaqah voluntary payment or good deed for charitable purposes that may be done at any time

salah prayer in the manner taught by Muhammad ﷺ, offered five times each day at set times

sanctity of life belief that life is holy or sacred

sawm fasting from just before dawn to sunset every day during the month of Ramadan

secular to do with everyday life and affairs of this world rather than religion

Shahadah 'declaration of faith' – 'There is no god except Allah and Muhammad is the Messenger of Allah'

Shari'ah 'the straight way' – Islamic law

Shaytan (Satan) 'rebellious one' – tempts people away from the path of Allah

Shi'ah one of the two main branches of Islam; Shi'ah Muslims believe that Ali was the rightful first successor (Imam) to Muhammad ﷺ and that 11 of his descendants succeeded him

shirk sin of believing in something other than Allah at time of a person's death

special revelation direct revelation about Allah to an individual or group, e.g. the prophets received special revelations and the Qur'an, Allah's final revelation, was revealed to Muhammad ﷺ; gives insights into the will or nature of Allah through, for example, a dream, vision, prophecy or experience

subha prayer beads used to help people keep count of their prayers

Sufi Muslim who tries to give up materialistic life and concentrates on the spiritual journey towards Allah

Sunnah the practices, customs and traditions of Muhammad ﷺ that are considered to be 'model' – a perfect example. They are found in Hadith and other texts

Sunni one of the two main branches of Islam; Sunni Muslims believe that Abu Bakr, Umar, Uthman and Ali were the rightful successors to Muhammad ﷺ

surah division of the Qur'an

talaq divorce

taqwa a Muslim's personal relationship with Allah and consciousness of Allah

tawaf circling the Ka'bah seven times anti-clockwise; a part of Hajj

Tawhid 'the Oneness or Unity of Allah' – Allah is the one and only universal God of all humanity

transcendent 'outside the created universe' – used to describe Allah as not limited by the rules of nature or time that affect human beings

Umar Muhammad's ﷺ father-in-law and second Khalifah

ummah the worldwide community of Muslims

Uthman the third Khalifah

wudu ritual washing that is part of the preparations for salah

Yathrib original name of Madinah

zakah 'welfare payment' – a percentage of wealth, if people can afford it, is given annually to benefit the poor

Zakat-ul-Fitr donations to those in need made at the end of Ramadan; usually represents the cost of a meal for each member of the donor's family

zulm wrongdoing against Allah, other people or yourself

Index

T

Tablighi Jama'ah 20
talaq (divorce) 81, 83
taqwa 37, 94
Taslim-Saif, Moona 50–51
tawaf 66
Tawhid 24, 25, 33
temptation 41, 44
terminal illness 45, 58–9
testing 4, 44, 57
transcendence 24, 28
transplants, organ 17

U

Umar 12, 17, 78
ummah 18, 22, 66–7, 70, 76, 94, 111
Uthman 17

V

Versi, Ahmed 84, 86

W

war 112–14
widows 86, 99
women 84–5, 93
  education of 6, 87
  and equality 5, 82, 83, 86, 87
work 4, 87
World Wide Fund for Nature 107, 109
wudu (ritual washing) 36–7

Y

Yathrib (later Madinah) 110, 111

Z

zakah (welfare payment) 12, 13, 22,
  98
Zakat-ul-Fitr 98
zulm 57